A Glittering

by

Robert J Brennan

For Lily and the memories so dear to me of the fun and laughter I was blessed to have shared with you.

Introduction

Robert John Brennan father of five children and 14 grandchildren was born and bred in Bootle, leaving the town in 1974, returning in 1984. Bobby was elected as a Labour councillor for the old Orrell ward his birthplace in 1994. Following boundary changes and the loss of a ward in Bootle he became one of the first Labour councillors to represent the new ward of Netherton & Orrell.

Bobby became the mayor of the borough of Sefton in the millennium year 1999/2000 a position that only one previous Labour councillor had held.

There is content that some readers may find offensive, particularly the use of certain expletives which are included in remaining true to the events and the characters, though Bobby has substituted a few spoken words.

Respice Aspice Prospice: Bootle motto 'look to the past, the present, the future'. The book is about the past, not so much about the present and certainly not the future which is somewhat difficult as you reach nearly three score years and ten. Dreams of what the future may hold now a matter of how long have I got left. The natural cycle of loss as we age when those that were ever present are no more and the words of my good friend Ralph ring loud and clear 'we are now occupying the front row seats' so I shall live each day in the present and time spent relaxing in our holiday home near Prestatyn North Wales and spending time to read the books I never found time to read.

I got the inspiration to write my book having read English poet Roger McGough of the Scaffold fame and his autobiography that I found fascinating more so through his local connection.

In my Liverpool home

As the famous song written by Peter McGovern and recorded by the folk group The Spinners goes "I was born in Liverpool down by the docks, my religion was catholic" well I was born in Walton hospital in Rice Lane Liverpool and spent my early years in my grandad & nanas house at 214 King Avenue in Orrell, being also my mother's childhood home. It was not down by the docks but you could see the dock cranes from the corner of the avenue due to its elevated position.

1

We lived closer to the grim walls of Walton prison now called HMP Liverpool which was opened in 1855. Its Victorian walls looking menacingly down over the field to the rear of King Avenue separated by the railway goods line from Canada dock, now filled in and at one with nature.

My childhood was one of joy and happiness of anger and despair were the Spector of penury loomed heavily over the home. Hunger and hardship measured through the eyes of a child in an ordinary working-class family were the main breadwinner was addicted to gambling.

I was born on the 19 October 1956 and lived in my grandad and nanas house in King Avenue Orrell until about 1960 when my parents were afforded their own home on the new housing development in Ford. I do not recall seeing much of my father during my early years as he was a ships steward in the merchant service. I recall him bringing me home a sheriff cowboy hat and Winchester rifle, not a real one I hasten to add. Nearly all of the memories are of my grandad and nana, the trips out to New Brighton, the gardens in Waterloo and the daily trips up the entry to Hollins sweet shop that sold the tastiest pink and white ice cream. My grandad Thomas McGaley worked in Reeds tin works in Orrell lane but was also a self-taught tailor and decorator and he gave to me my love of gardening.

My grandad grew bearded Irises, lily of the valley, and had a sprawling rambler rose named Albertine which I also have in my garden and geraniums which I think were one of his favourite plants that I also grow. Their distinctive smell reminds me of my grandad's lean-to that he built in King Avenue, bringing the garden into the house with its shelves enriched with scarlet geranium plants.

Religion

All of my grandparents were born to Irish immigrants that arrived in Liverpool at the turn of the twentieth century.

My paternal grandfather Robert Brennan born into an Irish Catholic family that settled in tenements in Reading Street off Scotland Road Liverpool.

My maternal grandfather Thomas McGaley born into an Irish Catholic family that settled in Marsh Lane Bootle. Robert Brennan married Elizabeth Brennan a Protestant and two large Irish families were joined together despite continuing religious differences. They had seven children all of whom were brought up under the Catholic faith.

Thomas McGaley married Isobel Thompson a Protestant they had two children one passed away in infancy and my mother their second child was also brought up under the Catholic faith.

I married Lesley McCallister a Protestant in Alexandra hall registry office in Crosby. For our two youngest children to be enrolled in St Robert Bellarmine Catholic school adjacent to our home we had to retake our wedding vows as our registry office marriage was not deemed a marriage sanctioned by the Lord. Enrolling them in St Robert Bellarmine school was nothing to do with having a Catholic upbringing as all our children were christened in the Church of England it was plain and simple convenient nothing more nothing less.

Unwanted residents in King Avenue

My mother told me that they would put vim or ajax powder around the bed legs so the cockroaches did not climb into the bed and each morning they would scatter across the floor when the light was put on. I don't recall seeing any at such a young age but when I represented Orrell ward in 1994 cockroach infestation was a regular complaint of constituents for many years till they decided to carry out systematic bating of whole terraces not just a complainant's home. I doubt very much that they have gone completely after all it is said they would survive a nuclear war.

We moved into neighbouring Marsh Avenue in November 1984 under the National Homes Exchange Scheme allowing you to move from one part of the country to another. However, for those accessing the scheme you had to accept that you would be offered houses in low demand. In other words what local applicants refused and to be fair why should you be given priority over those in local need. We were wholly ignorant of the cockroach problem that afflicted the area and on arriving at Marsh Avenue, we were met with half decorated walls and trades people all over the house. It was clearly not ready to be handed over and that first night the cockroaches were out in force.

3

The following morning my wife having captured one in a jar marched down to the area housing office taking also several eggs that resembled large jelly beans and demanded to see the area housing officer.

One of the junior housing assistants Stephen had lived by me in Ford and his brother was my form teacher Mr McShane in St Thomas Aquinas secondary modern school in Netherton. Stephen was quite apologetic and genuinely concerned unlike the senior housing officer who suggested my wife take the jar home and he will see her on Monday, this being Friday.

There followed the briefest of exchanges 'me take it home, I tell you what you take it home for the weekend and you look after it' Shortly afterwards it was agreed to re-house us on the Park Lane estate in Netherton and the cockroaches were exchanged for mice. The houses being terraced suffered frequent ingress that worsened when they pulled down Brabys on Bridal Road with the estate offering refuge.

Sefton pest control would repeatedly put bait under the floorboards and the sickening gas smell of the rotted corpses was awful. The Bootle Times got wind of the Marsh Lane house not being ready etc. and sent around a reporter and photographer. We were then told the editor was not too keen on the picture as amongst all of our piled-up furniture there was a microwave oven an obvious sign that the family must be slightly well off but the article did feature along with the microwave picture an assumed symbol of decadence.

I remember as a child in Simons Croft hearing mice running across my bedroom ceiling and my mother would say 'it is only birds' and I would say 'birds dont run they fly and would not be in the loft' not long afterwards we got our first cat.

There are flats in the corners of Simons Croft square and there was a mound of earth in the garden of one of the flats that we would use as a fort for our cowboy and Indian games and also to hide behind to plunder the loganberry bush in an adjoining back garden. One day we decided to excavate the mound and were surprised to find cockroaches including a white one that one of our mates swore was a lucky omen. Maybe it was as to the best of my knowledge no one ever reported seeing cockroaches in their home.

4

Back to King Avenue

In King Avenue we had a tin bath that was brought out into the back garden to double as a makeshift paddling pool surrounded by the irises and lily of the valley plants and scallop shells all in a row as in the nursery rhyme and could well have been written for my mother Mary, it wasn't of course.

My grandad had a small Murphy television set that had two knobs one for turning it on and off and one to turn it over from BBC to ITV. One of my favourite TV programmes was Rawhide that I would sit on the floor and watch whilst simultaneously playing with my two Wells Fargo stage coaches.

When my mother was at home she would not allow my grandad to bring me down to watch Rawhide and tell me it was the record by Frankie Laine that I could hear. Once my grandad brought me down as my mother had gone out but she returned almost at once having left her purse and there was hell to pay and I was sent back to bed.

My other favourite tv programme was Dr Who and the Daleks with William Hartnell. A programme that captivated me for many years and once led to a few of us walking to Waterloo and bunking into the emergency exit at the Classic cinema now known as the Plaza to catch glimpses of Dr Who and the daleks invasion of the earth with Peter Cushing. I say glimpses because we were routinely rounded up within minutes to the delight of the paid cinema goers and ejected as we shouted in defiance 'the films crap it's not even the real Dr Who'

Veterans of both world wars

My grandad would walk me up the entry to the shops and there was always a retired dock worker leaning on his gate and no matter how many times I went up that entry he would always be at the gate. His face looked rugged and he always had a cigarette in his mouth, wore the same grey jacket and red tie and regulation flat cap.

My grandad would always address him as Mr Flanagan and he would address my grandad as Tom.

'Good afternoon Mr Flanagan'

'Afternoon Tom, afternoon young sir' and I would just look up at him and cling to my grandad

I found out that Mr Flanagan was a veteran of the 'Great war' and had taken part in the battle of Ypres. My grandad a veteran of world war two and wounded at El Alamein the decisive battle that turned the tide of the war in the desert. He also fought in Italy with the Hampshire regiment at Monte Cassino his former Liverpool Kings regiment having taking massive losses in the desert.

I once sat watching 'All Our Yesterdays' with my grandad and it was an episode covering El Alamein and Tobruk and he showed me the medals that he would wear with pride each Remembrance Day at Bootle Kings gardens.

I remember him taking me to the service and I would stand and look up in awe of the bronze statues atop of the monument and would one day join Her majesties armed forces and lay my own wreath to the fallen. My grandad was proud of me in uniform but confided in my mum that he was worried he would see less and less of me and could not envisage his final years without me being a part of them. My grandad passed away not long after I became a councillor for his old stomping grounds and I recall when carrying his coffin to his final resting place in St Richards church yard in Skelmersdale telling him how much I loved and missed him and that love has never left me, my grandad is always close to my heart.I'm writing this part of the book on the second day of September 2024, my mother's birthday she would have been eighty-eight years old today but died on 21 June this year.

When my grandad passed away I was distraught but words from a former council colleague Eddie Mc lifted me so much when he asked about my grandad's wartime exploit. I told him of his being out on patrol in Italy and that he stumbled on crossing a small river dislocating his ankle. His colleagues helped him into the side of an overgrown part of the bank till they returned from patrol but they did not return they were ambushed and wiped out to a man. My grandad remained hidden for a few days then tried to get back to the British lines and found himself at an Italian farmhouse the occupants bandaged his ankle and hid him in a turnip store from an SS patrol. Had he of been discovered he along with them would have been summarily executed.

The kind and thoughtful words of Eddie Mc who said 'given your grandads war time experiences think how wonderful it was to have known and been loved by him' put his loss it into perspective and eased my heart ache.

As a local councillor I was invited to 238 Sqn TA barracks in recognition of having supported the changing of the street name leading to the Army reserve centre from Pelham drive to George Masters VC drive. The liaison officer Captain Tony Ravera a good friend told me of his intention to visit the Cassino war cemetery where his uncle rests having been killed in action at Cassino with the Hampshire regiment. He may well have been one of my grandads' band of brothers.

My Nana

My dear nana died when I was about six, she had brain cancer and is buried in the roman catholic part of Bootle cemetery. I went a couple of times as a child but there is no headstone nothing to say Bella McGaley rests here and that is something that I keep meaning to put right as I now hold the deeds to the plot. When my mother passed away I had hoped to lay her ashes with my nana but my youngest sister Joan born in 1963 was left our mothers ashes to dispose of and has her own plans. My sister Mary born in 1958 does not remember our nana but I'm blessed to have known and been loved by her. My youngest daughter Nicola gave birth to her first child Bella on 31 December 2023 and she has my nanas wedding ring that she will pass to Bella, the ring having been gifted to me by my mother.

My grandad was buried in St Richards in Skelmersdale as he re-married a wonderful lady June Pilling who had two sons Robert and Michael. June's first husband was in the 'forgotten army' the Chindits in Burma and she had many tales of her late husband's exploits up the Irrawaddy river behind Japanese lines.

My mother would never allow us to call June nana albeit she was our step nan. I guess no one could in my mother's eyes ever replace our nana and so we went through life sadly addressing her only as June.

June introduced us to the beautiful Isle of Man and the memories that it still holds for me. June and my grandad had a daughter Elizabeth who I think was born in 1964.

7

The council built a Roman Catholic school St Augustine's on the field that Mr Flanagan looked out across and once when I was playing for St Thomas Aquinas against the St Augustines a number of lads from the school were waiting to pounce on us at the end of the match which sadly heralded the years of violence directed at boys from another area when one of the would-be assailants recognised me and shouted 'Hey he is one of us from kingie ave'

And so, we were spared and allowed to go on our way up Southport road and freedom beyond. That of course was sadly very much the theme in the late 1960s early 1970s and coincided with the rise of skinheads 'bovver boys' as they were known in London and 'bovver' was their trademark.

St Augustines school was eventually bulldozed and became once again just a field though the far-right side of the field towards Keir Hardie Avenue now hosts a playing field and sports facility.

The geranium covered shelves in my grandads out building was later replaced with budgerigar nesting boxes as Junes eldest Mike bred them and they would occasionally be let out to fly around the outbuilding.

Mike married a young woman called Sarah and the nesting boxes soon took up residence in the bathroom of their Waterloo flat.

My grandad, June and Robert moved to the new housing development known as the Sefton estate which was said to be close to Sefton church. They lived in a top floor masionette at Pinfold Close now pulled down and from where you could see the spire of St Helens church in Sefton village.

My grandad kept a few of his prized geraniums in pots on the one small balcony which found themselves in direct competition for space during the summer months when washing was being aired on the wooden clothes horse.

My interest in gardens and plants and all things nature was developing and I   started working on my mother's rear garden in Ford, building a small rockery and planting crocuses to flower in spring.

My favourite shrub has to be Spirea douglasii with its tall rose-pink flowers that I helped my grandad move several from King Avenue to my mother's by handcart before he moved to the Sefton estate.

We also moved a Japanese cherry blossom that was in the front garden of King Avenue and painstakingly re-planted in the front garden in Simons Croft. Alas it was snapped in half by the window cleaner swinging his ladder around as he went into the flats next to us.

I do love spring and the first snowdrops but also Autumn for its blaze of rust coloured chrysanthemums and the old-fashioned pink Emperor of China, these are my favourite flowers of all time and herald the dark nights, bonfires and then Christmas. Even now at sixty-eight years of age I still look forward to my chrysanthemums first blooms though those same blooms announcing you are now another year older and one of the reasons why I felt compelled to write this book.

My paternal grandparents
I have many happy memories of my grandad Thomas McGaley, my nana Bella and my step nan June but none of my Father's parents who were always distant and cold towards us.

They lived in Grieve Road Fazakerley a very aptly named street as their house was a house of sorrow and great sadness.

On entering the living room your eyes would be moved to a large somber framed memorial over the fireplace

The Admiralty regrets to inform you of the loss of your son Able seamen John Brennan J942909 aged 23 years HMS Cossack who was buried at sea on 12 June 1959 in the waters off North Borneo. The memorial with its gold leaf had been commissioned by my grandparents and was the work of my uncle Brian Ward husband of my godmother Elizabeth (Betty) Ward nee Brennan.

Brian was an incredible artist who I believe also owned a violin shop and they lived off five ways in Childwall and we visited them a couple of times, it was another world, a huge house with apple trees.

The only other features in the dimly lit room in Grieve Road was a glass cabinet, that displayed Chinese crockery a feature of many seafaring homes. There was a lampshade on a cabinet that had a running waterfall on it. The bathroom was situated behind a curtain off the kitchen and the stairs immediately facing the front door.

The rear garden was large and bounded by overgrown privet hedges and large trees at the bottom. The garden borders were devoid of plants and the patio area was just dirty grey broken flag stones that stopped at a large wooden Green shed which was held together by a roof over rotted sides in which was kept an old redundant push mower, a pair of shears and a combination of rusting paint cans and small tins of lubricant oil. I shall revisit the shed later in the book, though it is undeserving of any mention.

Ford
The new housing estate built by Bootle corporation was bounded by Boundary Lane and Bootle golf course, Gorsey lane and the Leeds to Liverpool canal and Sterrix Lane with its convent of the good shepherd and Magdalene laundry.
You would regularly see barges carrying cork to the warehouse that went up in flames in 1964 its loading stage still visible today just under Cookson's bridge. There were two primary schools Holy Ghost and Sterrix Lane and St Lukes adult training centre at the top of Simons Croft. The houses were still being built when we moved in and there is a really informative book by former firefighter Syd Webster called 'Growing up in Ford' published in 2009 that covers the estate and some of its inhabitants.
I remember all the shops with the masionettes above now all gone with maybe one shop remaining. There was the chemist on the corner, Pearce wool shop then Vernon's stores a chandler. Next was Marshall and Weetch grocers, William Ross fruit and Veg, the Co-op butchers and a sweet shop that unlike others did not sell newspapers and next was the chip shop. In Simons Croft we would huddle around the one coal fire in the living room the only form of heating in the house but at least we had an indoor toilet and a proper bath and each morning my mother would sparingly place a few lumps of coal and fire lighters into the grate then a sheet of newspaper over the fire till the draught lit it up. The coal fire was later replaced by an electric fire with a decorated wooden surround that was supposed to resemble stone work but was just vinyl wall paper. The electric fire did not give off the same amount of heat but had an instant glow.

We had a Belfast sink which was replaced with an aluminum sink and dumped in a corner of the back garden but was utilised by me to keep tadpoles in. How things turn full circle with open fires and Belfast sinks now very much sought after.

My father left the merchant service and went to work in Jacobs biscuit factory in Long lane and at one period worked on the asphalt so I never really got to see him as a child due to his working patterns other than the odd Saturday when he would sit in front of the television watching the horse racing all day.

My grandad would come and do the decorating but my father put a stop to it as he 'was not having another man decorating his home' My mother thus did the decorating and would apply white leaded gloss paint to the living room ceiling with a two-inch brush dabbing over the countless drawing pins that were stuck on the ceiling from the paper Christmas decorations.

How I hated those yearly paint overs the smell would linger for days and your eyes hurt with the fumes. Years later I would cease to be bothered by lead paint or the dangers to one's health from the many carcinogenic substances in use. Despite the expulsion of my grandad we did still visit him each week taking the 56 bus from Sterrix Lane along Southport Road a journey I loved taking as it was leading me to my grandads and the warmth and care he gave to us. Excited we were to see the steam engines passing under the Netherton Way bridge on their way to Ford station and Aintree curve.

Hardship

I did not understand hardship but I knew what it was like to go without the things that other children had. There would be no queuing at the Walls ice cream van. I could only dream of the rocket lolly ices or the ice creams with their flakes and raspberry sauce.

My mother would buy a bottle of orange juice dilute it and pour it over some Disney character lolly ice figurines one being Yogi bear another favourite TV programme and serve them up as ice lollies.

Breakfast would be ready break porridge or cornflakes and one slice of toast and strawberry jam. For dinner we would have a boiled egg and a slice of toast. We would have beans but they were never Heinz and always tasted soapy.

I looked forward to the occasional chips and egg or chips with Spam and we were allowed one slice of white Wonderloaf bread to make chip butties and we would sometimes have corned beef hash that I would cover in brown sauce.

I would hear my father come home from work late bringing in a fish supper for himself and Chow Mein for my mother and I would fall asleep to the aroma drifting up the stairs. For dinner my father would be served one of his favourite dishes tripe and onions or salt fish and twice weekly lamb chops with mash and peas.

Me and my sister Mary would sit on the floor by the fire like dogs begging for food with the chosen one gifted the left-over chop to devour the morsel of meat or fat that was left on the bone. The prize went to whoever had been the best behaved as adjudged by my mother. Such was the hunger my sister Mary once eat leftover fishfingers off the cat's dish and scolded for having done so.

Begging for scraps reminds me of my time with MIND the leading mental health charity in England and Wales when a detained African patient who reported being hungry in the night as she watched staff gorge on Kentucky fried chicken and subsequently thrown a couple of chicken bones as 'you lot eat chicken' This was racism and abuse of a vulnerable person and the perpetrators were rightly sacked, though some of them were allegedly later employed by one of the managers who took up a post at a private psychiatric hospital.

Bedtime as a child was strictly before Coronation street started which along with Emergency ward ten were my mother's favourite programmes and woe betide if we tried to come downstairs during the airing of those shows.

'Mum can I get a drink of water'

'No get back in bed you should have got one before you went up'

'Mum can I go the toilet'

'No, you should have gone before you went up'

Resulting in wet pyjamas and my dad's black buckle belt which was usually administered on the Saturday before the horse racing came on.

The belt was kept on a shelf in my parents' room. I dreaded the words 'go and get my belt' with tears streaming down my face on each step I took till I picked up the instrument of 'Poena Corporalis ' My sister would plead with my father to stop, trying to grab his arm screaming 'stop it dad' and he would push her aside shouting 'do you want it as well' and then it was over and I had to take the belt back to its place of rest and welcome the peace and solace of my room.

One time I was so desperate I peed on the bedroom floor, the following day my poor cat Blackie just settling down on the bed was dragged by its fur screeching and lashed out the door, blamed for the pee smell in the room.

There was no taking a drink up to bed and I would creep into the bathroom and drink from the cold tap that was fed directly from the tank but at least it quenched my thirst.

I recall on a few occasions I ventured down the stairs instead of shouting down believing that If I came down I would have a better chance of getting a drink of water but those occasions only served to enrage my mother and she would drag me by the collar of my pyjamas and throw me out the front door.

Fortunately, we did have a small front garden and the old steel refuse bin store was next to the side door that led into the outhouse which my mother used as a dining room. I would squeeze in beside the bin amongst the cobwebs and stay there for what seemed like hours but it was for the duration of her TV programme.

Nearly all the other children in the square were still playing out after all it was only early evening and I would be spotted sneaking to the bin to the sounds of laughter 'ah look there's Brennan in his pyjamas' I would tell my mother that I was laughed at but she had no concern whatsoever for my embarrassment.

I was prescribed national health glasses for watching TV and every time my mother sent me to the closest neighbour for anything normally change for the electric meter so it never went out during one of her shows. I would have to wear the sodden glasses my embarrassment further sanctioned.

13

When that closest neighbour converted to the church of Jesus Christ of latter-day saints (Mormon) my mother ceased to send me there with them henceforth considered to be odd.

Childhood ailments
I was quite unwell as a child with German measles and also severe eczema and back and forth to Walton hospital, covered from head to toe in creams and though I escaped chicken pox I did suffer from shingles when I was in my thirties and was also acutely unwell with Scarlet fever requiring emergency hospital treatment.

Stafford Street Scallops
My mother would take us to her auntie Hettie's off Marsh Lane past the old timber yards and she would have scallops waiting for us which I would tuck into, no plates just the grease proof paper. I can see the green table cloth and brown teapot with the coloured knitted cosy and the bottle of brown sauce. Remembering also the white washed back yard walls and outside toilet with square shaped pieces of newspaper hanging on a piece of wire, the toilet just a circular hole in a slab of polished wood.
Another of my mother's relatives Kathleen worked in Woolworths in Stanley road and would give us sweets all free of course and those weekly visits to grandads and aunt Hetties sustained us. In order to supplement the meagre diet and in a quest to buy sweets I would routinely walk around the shops each day on the way to school looking for half pennies that may have been dropped in the gutter as you could get a half penny chew. Sometimes you found a three-penny bit but never a sixpence.
I would stare up at the jars on the shelves full of apple tarts, lemon cubes, chocolate eclairs, sweets of every description.
To be brought back to reality with 'Can I help you?'
'A half penny chew please' I would meekly reply.

Pocket money
We were never given pocket money as children and I was so envious of the other boys in the square that I once cried to my father and his blunt response was 'if all the other boys put their hands in the fire, would you?'

14

I pleaded with him tearfully over the next few weeks then he finally relented and said 'and how much pocket money do you expect?' I knew the other boys were getting half a crown so I asked for sixpence being a fifth of what the others received. The sixpence was handed to me but abruptly came to an end just three weeks later. I never got to ask him why but I guessed he may not have received pocket money as a child.

I tried to rationalise a reason and decided the meagre allowance was stopped because we had started to get a weekly comic the Beano for me and the Dandy for Mary so why would we also expect pocket money. How I loved to read the Bash Street kids, one of whom Plug had an uncanny resemblance to a local boy who was always referred to as Plug.

I would later change the Beano for the Victor and swap it with friends for their Eagle, Hotspur and Hornet comics, but I liked the Victor best with Alf Tupper the runner that lived on a diet of fish and chips. I once had a pen pal in America a boy called Larry Firkins from Sycamore, Illinois who is now a professor veterinarian and he would post me American boy scouting papers in return for the Victor that he said his Father loved to read. Eventually the pen pal writing ceased as most things do such as keeping in touch with friends you made on holiday.

When I was about ten a family member on my mother's side had a bread delivery round for Blackledge's bakery and I would help collect the bread money on a Friday night and Saturday morning and be gifted with an ice bun and half a crown that I would spend in Vernon's shop in Carr Meadow Hey on foreign stamps. At age fourteen I got my paper round and would buy myself the new football magazine the Shoot and cut out the pictures of Liverpool players for my bedroom wall.

Holy Ghost school

I cannot recall much of starting primary school, I was just four years of age but can still smell the polished parquet school hall floor. The distinctive smell of school mashed potatoes and cheese pie the Friday special that I detested along with its after's semolina. I wonder why I never looked forward to school meals as I was hardly at such a young age a discerning eater.

I had however developed an aversion to the slop that they dished out and it was rumored that the leftover slops were taken away to the piggeries as only a pig could delight in such cuisine. We were constantly reminded of the starving children in the world and how fortunate we were. No one would be allowed to leave the dining table till we had an empty plate. I once tried to hide the cheese pie under a dining seat but was caught and had to retrieve it and was given a note to take home the delivery of which had me sent straight to bed without any tea. I was spared the punishment that night as my father was working till ten o'clock at night in Jacobs but it would wait till the weekend.

I recall my teachers Mrs. Taggart who wore those cat-like glasses you see in 1960s American films, Mrs Charnley, Mr Taylor and Mr Simons my favourite teacher.

There was also Mr Sinnott and his banjo which he would play with gusto and shout loudly for me to show more enthusiasm as the class sang

'Brennan on the moor'

The class laughing and pointing their accusatory fingers in my direction as if I was the wee highwayman himself.

Willy Brennan (also known as John) displayed qualities of daring and gallantry and was immortalized in the ballad having met his fate at the end of a rope in 1804. My father was once presented with a framed family tree having been researched by a friend of his in Dublin and of course we were outlaws.

My own namesake Robert & John Brennan came across with the Irish volunteers to fight alongside William Wallace at the battle of Stirling what a glorious ancestral claim to fame. Nearly everyone in school had an Irish surname, we were all descendants of Irish immigrants. Yet today our heritage is not celebrated outside of St Patrick's day and orange lodge parades.

Liverpool it was once said had the largest Irish community outside of Ireland and Bootle was an Irish catholic enclave. As an equalities officer I supported Irish Community Care Merseyside in seeking to encourage Sefton residents to include their Irish heritage in the 2011 census. To include Irish alongside British because you cannot tailor services to meet the needs of the community if that community is invisible.

This is important when we consider health care as many people of Irish descent including myself are carriers of the mutant Irish gene that leads to Haemochromatosis an iron overload that affects one in five Irish people and can often skip a generation.

Football

I played for the Holy Ghost school team as a right back despite my diminutive size but sadly lost my place. The hurt I experienced when going to the class room door where the team sheet was pinned up to see my name omitted. The shame I felt and how on earth will I tell my dad I was dropped. I need not have worried my hurt and shame were for me alone he acknowledged my despairing words with a shrug of his head then returned to the racing page of his newspaper, no words of comfort were afforded me.

I would however play football again for St Thomas Aquinas school and Sunday league football for The Tailors Arms aka Cookson's.

I was often summoned into the head teacher's office for extra reading lessons and I always seemed puzzled why I should require them, was I not one of the brightest in the class? seemingly not.

There was a large gold fish pond situated just outside of the assembly/dinner hall in the Holy Ghost school that could only be accessed through the glass doors in the hall. Sometimes we would be allowed through to gaze in wander at the large gold fish swimming among the white and rose flowering lily pads. Thriving in a more natural environment compared to the poor specimens that you would win at the fair and bring home in a plastic bag to perish in a glass bowl after a week or so.

Lunch time period

I found primary school very lonely at times especially when my class mates went home at dinner time or lunch as it is known today.

I would be lost after struggling to eat the school meals the scooped mash, cheese pie and semolina and would take myself off to the side of the school and venture into the sand pit with its red fire ants.

Armed with a stick I would disrupt the colonies then make a hasty retreat as they swarmed out to assault the attacker and did their bites hurt.

You wore short trousers and a balaclava that kept your ears warm but when it was exceptionally cold you had to try and huddle in the corner of the entrance door to the school corridor whilst the teacher would shout his annoyance.

'You boy out of there, go and play'

'I have no one to play with sir' and so I would be cast out into the cold waiting for the clock to strike one to end the boredom and herald the warmth of the class room.

'Sir I need to go the toilet'

'No, you don't' would be the response

'But I do sir'

'Away with you'

'But I need the toilet'

'Out of there Brennan'

'But sir' my words fading away.

Occasionally a kind spirited lunch time assistant would allow you in the building and you would make for the first radiator to thaw out.

I found most of the male teaching staff to be devoid of any empathy for the suffering of us mere mortals because it was their turn to do lunch duty.

I recall one teacher his face beaming with delight as the girls flocked to hold his hand at breaktime which in full flight resembled the Angel of the North with its outstretched arms being the girls linking each other either side of sir and marching around the playground, all very strange indeed.

Size doesn't matter

Being small for my age, some boys would ridicule my age and others would be protective of me which I was not really in need of as I could scrap with the best of them. Once a boy from another school who I played with said his father told him he had to play with boys his own age

On my eight birthday an older boy came over to me pointing and laughing

'Why are you wearing that badge, you're not eight'

'Yes, I am it's my birthday today'

18

'No, it's not'
'Yes, it is, I should know' at which I received a punch on the nose.

I could feel my eyes watering, I was starting to cry and aware of others laughing as the teacher pushed other pupils out of the way and escorted me into the building. I knew then that I was not going to let that happen again and so I spent my school years defending my honour or rather my stature and defending other boys who were being picked on, I guess even then I was standing up for the underdog.

Escape
One day I had enough of the school and set off to my grandads, there was no fences and locked gate so I simply walked out and proceeded to King Avenue.

I got as far as the annexe building at the top of Boundary Lane which was also being used by Sterrix lane school when I was stopped by Mrs Hillen the crossing lady 'and where do you think you are going'
'To my grandads' I replied
'No, you are most certainly not' and I was ushered into the school gates.

The Holy Ghost school was called and shortly afterwards a teacher arrived to return me to school. I later heard my Mother telling a neighbour 'the little bugger knew which way to get to his grandads'. Another time I left school and went along the canal to Litherland tip to look for Brooke Bond PG tips books, as a boy in class had brought in two books he had found whilst searching the tip with his brother.

I entered the canal at Swifts lane and got as far as Cookson bridge when a man out fishing said 'what are you doing on here, get off home'.

Walking nonchalant into the square to shouts of
'Here he is now' and my mothers' 'wait till your father gets home'.

I was totally oblivious to all the fuss but as it was around the time of the infamous moors murders I must have driven my poor mother out of her mind.

The Annexe

The Holy Ghost year four was situated in the old anti-aircraft battery barracks situated at the top of Boundary Lane at the junction with Sterrix Lane and became known as the annex.

The class rooms were old brick and wooden billets with a single stove in the middle. The caretakers house was the old commanding officers' billet and the playground was of course the drill square.

There were two aircraft shelters to the side of the barracks, one of which was allegedly home to an elusive down and out that we affectionately named Ted the tramp and of course Ted was never spotted.

The likely occupants were foxes as parts of countless parts of rabbits were found in there and the golf course was a haven for rabbits.

Left by the wayside

There was a rather unkempt boy even by those days standards who was given the alias of Ted and who was forever being told to stand in the dunce corner.

The teachers would shout 'dunce corner now'

'You are thick boy what are you?'

'Thick sir' at which the class would erupt into laughter.

'You are a disgrace boy can't your mother darn your clothes?'

More hilarity filled the class room and instead of lessons he would be sent outside to pick litter off the playground or sweep up the autumn leaves.

There was no special educational needs assessments and he was being failed by a system that did not care, left by the wayside.

On one occasion we were walking home across the hill to Simons Croft having been looking for skylarks' nests with egg collecting then a pastime of many boys. We watched as Ted started throwing bottles down the entries that separated each terrace house allowing access to the rear gardens.

Why on earth he decided to behave like this was never established but he would launch a bottle down each entry as he made his way past the row of terraces facing the field. We gazed open mouthed at the spectacle and as he was getting to the end of the terrace his final bottle missed the entry and sailed through the living room window to shrieks and screams from within.

We made our way down the hill and gave in his name to the shocked and enraged residents, who were fortunately unhurt as Ted whooping loudly disappeared down Broad Hey.

We never saw Ted again till he turned up in St Thomas Aquinas school some four years later and was placed in class three -four D the dunce classes a mixture of year three and year four pupils all extremely vulnerable and likely to struggle on leaving school. Looking back there did not appear to be any additional support for them as they would idle their days in the science lab feeding the white mice and whatever else was kept in there while the teacher sat back, feet up on the desk reading his newspaper.

Boundary Lane

The top half of the field on Boundary Lane opposite the golf course was littered with parts of houses and may well have been from the blitz but I was never able to establish the origins of the rubble. You would see skylarks soaring high up in the sky and the melody was a common sight to behold and hear over Boundary Lane and the golf course and yet we collected eggs not realising that one day those skies would be empty of lark song.

I loved to collect Brooke bond tea cards such as British birds and butterflies.

'Mum can you get more tea'

'No, we are getting t-bags from now on' so I never got to complete a Brooke Bond album but I do now have several complete albums to remind me of the good things I enjoyed and could not obtain as a child. We would wait for weeks to loan out the ladybird book of garden birds and other bird books in the school library. Some boys would take empty nests and place them in bushes in their own gardens and claim a Blackbird or Song thrush had nested there.

Not quite a kestrel

One afternoon I climbed up a rather large hawthorn tree that bounded the school perimeter and caught a starling fledgling that I intended taking home as a pet. Not dissimilar to the exploits of Casper the young boy in the Ken Loach film Kes that was doing the rounds in the late 1960s. That film brilliantly captured life and school days in a working-class town and my life echoed that of the film. I also had a paper round and would sit and read the comics before delivering them often removing the occasional toy gifts and of course I would go nesting.

Having captured the fledgling I put it in my duffle bag which I then placed under my desk in the classroom.

The banjo came out and the class started singing the usual songs which was interrupted by chirping and fluttering from somewhere in the class.

'Can anyone hear a bird'

'No sir' I would eagerly respond.

'There it goes again, Brennan it's by you'

'It's you Brennan you have got a bird in your desk'.

'I haven't sir' I replied quickly pulling apart the draw string of my duffle bag at which the starling fledgling made its flight for safety and proceeded flying around the class room with droppings everywhere.

'You boy open that window, you open that door, get me that brush so I can chase it out'.

Eventually the saga ended and the bird flew out one of the now open windows.

'Who brought that bird in, was it you Brennan?'

'No sir' at which one of the class room snitches pulled a face at me and said 'he had it in his bag sir'.

On inspection my bag was awash with bird droppings and along with a note from the school I had to reveal the much-soiled bag to my mother.

There would be no blue Peter for me, no dinner, straight to my room where I remained until the following morning.

My mother blamed my interest in birds' eggs as the problem for my behaviour in school 'Just look at the state of that duffle bag, well you can sodden well clean it' and ' just wait till your father comes home' following which she unleashed her fury on my head with an awesome clout and then my prized birds egg collection that she pummeled with her fists and dumped in the bin'

Enemy soldiers

When I first started school the dinner break boredom was eased by a junior boy who would make sure us little uns were okay and he would warn us of the dangers of the red fire ants in the sand pit and tell us cats would use it as a toilet.

He would tell us war stories and that Japanese soldiers were behind a hillock across the lane. No one ever thought to think that the war had ended and no enemy troops ever landed in England least of all the Japanese but his stories kept me and whoever else captivated.

'Dad there's Japanese soldiers on the hills by the school'. He would not turn his head from his newspaper so I never got to know if the Japanese troops were there or not.

Many years later that older boy Henry came into the solicitor's office where I worked in Netherton seeking help for a family member of his.

He of course knew who I was as I was also a local councillor

'Hello Robert it is so good to see you, how well you have done'

'It is so good to see you too I replied' It was like meeting an old long-lost friend which I guess he was. I don't think he would ever know how he had saved me during those often-lonely school dinner breaks.

First school friend

My first school friend was called William and he lived in flats facing the field alongside Boundary lane and I would go to his after school to play and for tea. He would lend me his comic 'The Treasure' and I would be transported to a farm and the animals and birds that made the farm their home.

Williams father would take us to Formby beach in his little van and we would marvel at the army lorries heading to Altcar rifle ranges, proclaiming one day we will be soldiers. Then out of the blue his Mother informed me that they were moving to Formby but I was welcome to visit William anytime but I never did.

As Mayor of Sefton in 1999 I took my grandson Michael and my two youngest children Nicola and Andrew to Formby for the Dickensian day and whilst chatting to the attendants I heard a voice 'Mr Mayor you will not remember me but you went to school with my son Billy but you were both infants'

I did remember and said 'Mrs Dunne' she smiled at my remembering and said 'yes and Billy will be here soon'

I remember William as having blonde curly hair and then there he was with his blonde curly hair walking towards me. I held out my hand and said 'William' and he took my hand in his simply saying 'Bobby' we had never forgotten that first friendship.

The Queens shilling

Not the one given to recruits to the armed forces but the one that bought a school dinner. One winter when I was about ten I apparently slipped on the ice in the drill hall playground and awoke at home, puzzled to see the clock on top of the television set with its fingers indicating school was over.

My mum told me that I was brought home by Mr Sinnott of the banjo fame as I had slipped on the ice and fainted.

I could not make sense of any of it and had lost my memory of that day and it never came back.

On the Monday my mother sent me off to school with strict orders to reclaim the shilling dinner money for last Friday when I had fainted.

I walked into the secretary's office.

'Hello Robert how are you now'?

'I'm okay now '

'That is good, how can I help you'?

'My mum told me to get the shilling for last Friday dinner'

'You had your dinner' she replied, I of course had no clue and relayed the message to my mother.

'Well did you eat your dinner or not?' asked my mother

'I don't know I can't remember' I replied

'You must know if you ate your bloody dinner'

'I dont remember mum'

My mother had to reluctantly admit defeat, reminding me that money doesn't grow on trees with the customary clout around the head.

I once said 'Bloody hell' when losing at a game of marbles and a local snitch ran and knocked on my house door

'Mrs Brennan your Bobby has just said a swear word'

I was immediately summoned over to the house watched by all the kids in the square gathering around the house gate and protested that I had only said bloody and that the word bloody is in the bible. I was summarily whacked about the head and dragged in for the rest of the day.

School milk monitor

I was proudly made a school monitor along with my friend Paul and we would be allowed to leave the class just before the end of lesson to deliver the daily half bottle of milk to the classes. We would pile the crates onto a trolley that we would push up and down the corridors delivering the milk and collecting the empties.

One morning we drove at speed down the corridor and just before we reached the couple of steps that led down to the reception area we applied the trolley brake but the noise of the crates clattering on the trolley disturbed the classes and out came the teachers

'You boys what on earth are you doing?'

'Delivering the milk sir'

'Well make less noise about it'.

However, it all came crashing down around us one morning.

We were heading for the end of the corridor and about to apply the brake when Father O'Donoghue the parish priest appeared out of nowhere.

His sudden appearance broke our concentration sending us and the trolley over the steps with the crates of milk launched across reception.

Fortunately, we were unhurt but got a right ear bashing off the priest who grabbed us by our shirt collars and whacked us around the head demanding that we are stripped of our monitor position with which the head teacher promptly complied.

It would be another four years before me and Paul were given any position of trust again but that was at a different school and for later in the book.

Those small free milk bottles were welcomed though one time the milk tasted vile and I noticed something black in the bottle, which turned out to be a piece of rubber. I had to drink all the milk, you were not allowed to speak, just sit still until the bottle was empty. If it had of been a favourite teacher I would not have hesitated in raising my hand, but such was not my luck that day.

University challenge

Around the final year of primary school, I befriended and sat with a boy called Peter who had come to the Holy Ghost from St James in Bootle and is now the MP for Bootle.

We would challenge the two boys behind us to a daily quiz competition that we of course never failed to lose as Peter would bring in a volume of the encyclopedia Britannica and off we would go with our own version of University challenge.
'We are first, right who is the president of Botswana?'
'What'
'Who is the president of Botswana?' 'We don't know' was the reply'
'Ha, ha it is Seretti Gottenberg Mophri Kharma'
'That's a daft question, our turn, who did Johnny Haynes play for?'
'Fulham, our turn again when was the poor law?'
'We don't know' '1834' we replied smirking
'Okay then where did Davey Crockett die?' 'The Alamo' I said turning to Peter and adding went to see it with my dad John Wayne was in it.
And so, it continued till they eventually conceded defeat, we would get 2-3 wrong but they failed to get a single answer right.
The irony however in that both contestants Jeff and Alex passed the eleven plus and went to Salesian college while me and Peter failed the exam and went to St Thomas Aquinas secondary modern.
As a teenager I would sit with my friends outside the Carr Meadow Hey shops in Ford having formed our own estate gang which every area now boasted. We were not 'bovver boys' we were just school friends that hung out together chased girls, listened to music and followed our beloved Liverpool or Everton.
One evening Ted of the bottle throwing fame suddenly appeared and was summarily mocked and about to be sent packing when he asked if we wanted fish and chips which of course we accepted without asking were the money had come from.
We were treated to fish and chips for about three nights over the next few weeks when the question was finally posed.
'Hey Ted where do you get all the money from?'
'I deliver papers to the ships on the dock road' Ted replied
I had my own paperbound that paid about £1.15 per week plus regular tips and said 'you can't be paid that much delivering papers'.

Teds response knocked us all for six in that he revealed masturbating the men on the ships for a fiver a go.

He was immediately covered in whatever fish and chips remained.

One of our gang being a neighbour of Teds family went immediately to report the shocking revelation after which he was taken into care and I never knew what became of him. There were of course a few miscreants on the estate that would see the inside of reform school and Borstal.

One summer we sat again by the shops and were treated to a day out to New Brighton, trip over on the ferry, hours on the fare and burgers in the Wimpey bar, no questions asked. We learnt later that our benefactor had stolen his father's entire work mates Christmas club savings or tontine as it was referred to then which he was responsible for collecting and with-it being August it was a tidy amount. Despite there being thefts from gas and electric meter boxes always by a family member and the occasional break in at the adult training centre to steal ice cream there was no burglaries of the residential homes or even garden sheds and you could go on holiday if rich enough to do so.

Once when my mother had gone out to the bingo, the electricity went off and I reached for the two-shilling piece off the mantlepiece and after inserting the coin into the slot went back into the living room to watch the TV and realised to my immediate horror that I had put one of my foreign coins in the meter by mistake but it had worked. Now given the absence of pocket money I pocketed the two-shilling piece and periodically used the rest of my foreign coins never expecting the ploy to be uncovered when one day the electric man came around to empty the meter.

I had overheard my mother telling a neighbour she expected a rebate and would be going to get her hair done. The shriek of horror when the coins were deposited on the table there being no rebate. My remaining coin collection all too small for the meter was dumped unceremoniously in the bin along with a large medallion that I had found when exploring the piggeries at the rear of the Tailors Arms pub better known as Cookson's.

The medallion had the Liverpool coat of arms on it and said Lord mayor of Liverpool.

I recall bringing it in to show my father who looked at it with disinterest before returning to his newspaper so I never got to know what it was. The piggeries were built on a former Victorian dump that people would go and dig up bottles. I once took some of my children there and dug up several Victorian clay pipes.

Tailors Arms public house

Not many people know the origin of the Tailors Arms pub that was better known as Cookson's after the licensee Jimmy Cookson and his father old Jimmy Cookson who raced pigeons and kept them at the rear of the pub.

The pub now renamed Cookson's bridge, the bridge however has a commemorative stone on it that states Gorsey Lane bridge opened 1935 or 1937 I'm not sure of the date.

I played right back for the Tailors Arms for several seasons and was managed first by Tommy Hill and later by Harry Maguirk who ran the betting shop situated near to the back of the pub. We would play at Buckley Hill and Litherland Moss playing fields. How I would hate turning up to find that the match was postponed due to a frozen pitch. There were so many aspiring players who never made the professional grade but played amateur league.

Sunday Mass

I hated having to attend Sunday mass and the Saturday confession to be absolved of your sins so you could receive communion. Every Saturday lunchtime we would file into the Holy Ghost church which stood on the corner opposite the school, a really large building now replaced by a small housing development. The new church situated in the grounds of the school much smaller and likely a sign of diminishing worshippers.

There would be two confessional boxes one for Father Laing and another for Father O'Donoghue who also took mass at St Monica's.

You would be sat there waiting for the confession box to be vacant hoping and literally praying 'please lord let it be Father Laing and not Father O'Donoghue'

My prayers went unanswered I always got Father O'Donoghue.

So, in I went 'bless me father for I have sinned it has been two weeks since my last confession'

28

'What! two weeks, two weeks' would be the roar from the other side
'Why has it been two weeks, you're a boy you will have sinned, you have sinned haven't you?'
Quickly thinking I replied 'yes Father'
'Well get on with it then'
'Bless me Father'
'You have said that get on with it I haven't got all day'
I could not think of any sin that I had committed so I said
'I have given cheek to my mother and told lies' the latter being the lie I was now telling.
'Given cheek to your mother, did our lord savior give cheek to his mother?'
'No father'
'No, he never and only the devil tells lies.
I was given five our Fathers and three hail Mary's as my penance and so, I was absolved to go to eleven o'clock mass on Sunday.
I hated that mass there was a woman that looked and dressed like Hyacinth Bouquet of keeping up appearances fame and she would usher all the children up to the front. No matter how many times you crept in at the back you would see her pacing up and down the aisles in her round blue hat looking for late comers. Then you were nabbed and frog marched up to the front rows to remain seated till mass finished, no chance of an early exit.
Once I must have been laughing and unfortunately caught Father O'Donoghue eye as when kneeling down to receive communion Father O'Donoghue hit me hard in the forehead with his knuckle and moved the altar boy on to those more deserving of the host.
The incident was inevitably reported back to my parents through another child's parents and I was grounded for a week albeit my parents were not church goers themselves.
I was able to escape the dreaded eleven o'clock mass when I got my paper round and would reluctantly attend four o'clock mass in the grounds of Ford cemetery the entrance to the chapel was via a door in Sterrix lane.
I was once watching the Sunday afternoon matinee 'The sands of iwo Jima' with John Wayne my film hero whilst the clock counted down to four o'clock.

I was hoping that my father would allow me to watch the rest of the film and tell my mother that I can go to mass next week.

I was to be disappointed in that when my mother said 'mass now you're going to be late' my father remained silent and so I trudged off to mass and never got to see the raising of the flag at mount Surabachi.

The Holy Ghost had a school gala each year and a parent I think a Mr Twist would always have the best prizes once a pair of chipmunks.

As pupils it was expected that we all attend to support the event but though I would attend I never had any money to spend so would wander around staring at the stalls.

Once as teenagers we tried to take the gala stalls from the back of the church for bonfire wood when the new priest Father Coffey came around

'You boys what on earth are you doing?'

'We are collecting bonfire wood Father'

'No, no, no you cannot take these, they are for the gala'.

At the same time two boys we knew that attended Warwick Bolam school were crossing Swifts lane bridge and we said

'It was them father they said it was okay'

Father Coffey shook his fist at them shouting 'Protestant heathens'

To be returned with the two-finger salute and the immortal words 'Fuck off'

We could hardly contain ourselves and burst out laughing when out of ear shot of Father Coffey.

Father Coffey once pedaled into the square on one of his visits to the parishioner's and out came the club biscuits and tea. A treat that me and my sister had to literally beg for, more about that later?

Did you notice the difference in church today it being quite cold outside?'

'Erm no father my mother replied'

'So, you never noticed the heating was back on?' it having been broken for several weeks with multiple complaints of the cold church.

'Oh yes father it was quite snug' replied my mother.

Then came the decisive blow 'tell me now why has there been no parish fund envelope for some time?'

The room fell silent and a few seconds later Father Coffey said 'Well I shall leave it with you, thank you for the tea and broken biscuit'.

The story did not end well for Father Coffey as he went to two further houses in the square and came out the last house to find his bike had two flat tyres and stripped of its bell and pump. It was not long before the culprit was named, and it was a Protestant boy who had bartered the bell and pump for a puncture repair to his own bike.

There was a Jewish boy on the estate that built a lucrative business building and repairing bikes and he was probably an original entrepreneur and the go to person for repairs and quite reasonable. He later went onto repair motor bikes and cars, being self-taught it was some achievement.

His father always sported a black royal tank regiment beret having served in the desert war. He would follow the rag and bone man's cart around the estate collecting the horse droppings for future manure for his rhubarb plants.

'Scrap any old iron'

You would look out and there he was with a window cleaning bucket and spade following the cart. There were a couple of Jewish families on the estate and if anyone mentioned one of the boys they would always be referred to by their first name followed by the Jew.

Racism

I think back to the television programmes of the day and racist sitcoms with my first recollection being of 'Till death us do part' introducing us to Alf Garnett' who spent every episode spouting vitriol about black people and extolling the glories of the British Empire and how 'Old Enoch was right'. Every episode dominated with grossly offensive words. Liverpool people would be described less offensively as a mixture of Chinese Micks. The 1970s were also dominated by similar programmes 'It aint half hot mum' being just one of them and extremely popular but I could not see how people found derogative terms funny.

Likewise, 'The comedians' with some ridiculing their own race for the sake of laughs from a white British audience Why on earth were some people gifted their own show for being racist bigots.

I remember once my mother talking to a neighbour about Coronation street and a new character who was a black bus driver and sacked because of lies told by one of the shows main characters Len Fairclough and his unpaid fare.

My mother and the neighbour were more shocked at the inclusion of a black family in the show than the storyline.

I remember getting the bus to Skelmersdale to see my grandad and on getting off the bus at what was then Cross keys in Grimshaw lane the first thing I noticed was the letters NF on a wall.

An image that remains ingrained in my mind its ideology an evil I would campaign against for all of my life.

Standing on the kop I would hear racist chants directed at black players such as Clive Best who played for West Ham. In 1972 when cutting through Stanley park after Liverpool played Birmingham city I saw two Birmingham fans one black the other white being attacked by local youths.

As they tried to run away one youth shouted 'leave him get the N' using a derogatory word.

That incident sticks with you like you have just witnessed something very evil and of course you just had.

In the Bootle and Litherland district junior football league there was a brilliant black player but as with the Jewish boys on our estate he would also be referred to by his first name followed by a derogatory term.

My father expressed discriminatory views as did his youngest brother Tony and both would pour scorn on my work as an equalities officer saying 'You are allowing all these to terrorists to come into the country' and claiming that
'We will all have to go to Mosque soon'

My Uncle Tony would tell me that 'my father would turn in his grave if he had one' because of my support for asylum seekers and refugees and he would say 'you should be ashamed of yourself' call yourself an English man. I would simply laugh, it was pointless trying to argue with either my uncle or my father as they held such entrenched views.

Travellers

As a child I witnessed abuse and hatred of the Traveller community when Irish Travellers would stop on the field on Boundary Lane and remain for a few weeks.

Their presence always resulted in gangs of older youths throwing stones and bottles at them and eventually Bootle council placed high mounds of earth around the field to prevent access.

People always complain about Travellers stopping temporarily on land or car parks. The solution is in the provision of transit sites but though identified in the Sefton council local plan for many years at the time of writing this book the authority has still not provided any.

I once had an article printed in 'Traveller Times' about an incident in Southport were a former Lib-Dem councillor was calling for the prosecution of travellers that had allegedly broken the law in gaining access to a closed site.

The article featured in the local press leading to disgusting racist comments on social media. I challenged the councilor to condemn the hate crime comments one of which suggested take a can of petrol to the Traveller site which I reported to Merseyside police as a hate crime.

However, my challenge to that councillor was ignored and Travellers continue to be the last bastion of acceptable racism.

Those high mounds of earth became a well-trodden path that we gave the name Wibbly Wobbly Way after a children TV programme of the time called Willy Wombat and we all adopted the names of the characters. I of course was Willy Wombat and Paul my milk monitor friend was Dolly.

After we left Primary school the names were dropped other than for Paul who continued to be addressed as Dolly even during football matches you would hear 'Dolly over here' 'Dolly pass it' and it just stuck and Paul was totally unfazed by it.

The only objection came from Paul's mother when we once knocked for him. 'Is your Dolly in' 'don't call him Dolly' would be the reply and we would look at each other puzzled?

'Paul your friends are here' Paul would appear then it was 'Hi Dolly you coming out'

East is East

There was an incident involving an Asian family that I include purely because it reminds me of the film East is East with Om Puri who played George the Asian chip shop owner.

In 1972 Idi Amin the brutal dictator that ruled Uganda expelled Ugandan Asians from the country many of whom sought refuge as UK passport holders.

One Ugandan Asian family settled in Musker Drive, their home next to an entrance to lock up rented garages from where you could access St Mary's Grove.

One Saturday morning my friend Barry who lived in St Mary's Grove came to mine and as he had forgotten something we started back to his house.

We rounded the corner and on the side garden wall of the Ugandan family's house was painted in large white letters PAKISTAN.

The youngest member of the Ugandan-Asian family was called Stanley and was kicking a ball against the painted wall. Barry had not spotted the graffiti on coming to mine and said to Stanley 'Hey when did that happen?'

'Dunno' said Stanley at which point his father appeared

'You' did this?'

'No, we never, we have only just seen it'

'Why these bastards write Pakistan we are Indian not Pakistan'.

Instead of just walking away Barry pointed at young Stanley and said

'Maybe it was because his name is Stan and they thought you were Pakis' adding 'you know Paki Stan' at which Stanley was grabbed by the ear lobe and marched inside the house to shouts of 'So, it is your fault'.

We stood there frozen to the spot when suddenly the father burst out the front door hurried down the path and gave young Stanley's ball a great big kick sending it off down the road before going back in slamming the door.

Early years in Ford

I recall there would be stone throwing and name calling as catholic school children from Holy Ghost and protestant children from Sterrix Lane would over a period of days have running battles 'catty cats' 'prody dogs' which was bizarre as we all lived in the same street. It never carried on at home only on the way to and from school but it thankfully petered out to be replaced by street wars.

We would declare war on Hampshire Avenue but they once occupied the square waving a large Union Jack flag which signaled our defeat.

The Hampshire's built a swamp on the field that ran alongside the canal and caught one of our numbers and tossed him in. He crawled out looking like he had fell in a vat of treacle.

That was the final straw so we marched around with our allies from Buckingham close and Westmoreland Avenue.

We far outnumbered the Hampshire's who retreated from their swamp and launched bricks at us from the safety of their gardens one of which landed on my head causing a split that required several stitches.

That single act signaled a lasting peace with future campaigns fought on the football pitch on the 'Greenie' now the site of South Sefton sixth form with many a cup competition held throughout the summer months.

Our team consisted of eleven boys from the square aged between 9 and 13 with lads from other streets guesting for us. We would regularly return victorious from our matches against Hampshire Avenue, Randall Drive and Buckingham close though the latter always ended in punch ups.

Two of our team were brothers Alvin and David Martin, Alvin was my next door neighbour and we would have heading competitions across the back fence and he went on to play for West Ham and represent England. Alvin once told me that his father thought I was a really good footballer but I think my speed down the wing gave the illusion I was better than what I was. I could knock a ball past an opponent and run with it and not be caught, crossing it was however the problem.

We had another lad in the team who oddly supported Man City and nicknamed Mercer after the Man City manager of the day.

I did go onto represent St Thomas Aquinas school in cross country, 4 by 100 metre relays and the 1500 meters and came second in the Bootle schools' athletics to the delight of our sports teacher as we accrued enough points to win the overall trophy.

Not a lot of good things were said about that school but it excelled in football and athletics.

Holy Ghost cubs

I was never really interested in the cubs and they only became of interest to me when one break time in school one of my friends Alex of the defeated university challenge and himself a cub told us of Tawd Vale and that birds of all sorts nested there.

That was it I was hooked and joined which meant my mother taking me to Jack Sharps to get the green top, cap and rest of the paraphernalia woggle etc.

I did go to Tawd Vale which was a bit of a disappointment to me as we had to remain in our respective packs and not wander off.

My Mother had made me a shed load of spam butties most of which were fed to the ducks.

I hated 'bob a job week' having to perform good deeds like shop for a neighbour for sixpence a deed and a 'job done' sticker in their window.

I left the cubs not long after we were summoned to attend the opening of the new Roman Catholic cathedral 'Paddy's wigwam the whole day dragged.

There was an elusive gang the Walsh's that were rumored to frequent the hills though no one ever seen them but it was a concern for us cubs walking home.

Once two of us were walking past the hills and noticed a group of boys on bikes at the top of the hill.

'That must be the Walsh's' said my friend Stephen at which point we decided to drop our short trousers and moon them.

There followed threats of imminent death and they set off to cycle down the hill so we legged it into Northumberland Avenue and dived behind a garden hedge and heard them cycling around calling to each other.

We remained motionless for about 15 minutes then emerged from our hiding place and made our way home.

Had we met the Walsh's we never knew but either way we had lived to tell the tale.

Mentioning the RC cathedral there was a very large mosaic of the Holy Spirit on the wall of the old Holy Ghost church and it was transferred to the cathedral when the old church came down and is situated to the right of the altar.

When I was the Mayor of Sefton I did as all Mayors before me visit Tawd Vale and I was introduced to the Northwest area officer Peter Morgan who was a scout in Holy Ghost and I did remember him.

Next time I seen Peter he was a director at Sefton council and though I cannot recall the incident it was reported back to me that Peter was regaling them of when I joined the cubs and his informing me that he was my sixer to receive the reply 'Not for fucking long you're not'

My venture in the cubs lasted only a few weeks to my mother's anger having had forked out on the uniform so it does fit with the short time span.

Birthdays

I only ever recall having one birthday party when I was about ten years old I had a few friends in the square but they were often scorned upon by my mother who had fallen out with their mothers for whatever reason. There were little cliques in the square and if you fell out it with one you fell out with them all.

One day I arrived home from school to be asked by my mother who are you best friends and I replied naming my three best friends in the square. They are not your best friends she retorted and nothing more was said.

A few days later it was my birthday and on arriving home from school I was ushered straight upstairs to get washed instead of just sitting down and   playing with my cat Blackie that was walking in and out of my legs.

When I came down she said follow me and opened the outhouse door for me to be greeted with 'happy birthday' and what a surprise none of my three best friends were there only the friends my mother believed I should have.

The following day I had great difficulty in explaining to my real friends that I knew nothing of the party and of course I was not invited to their birthday parties.

I was once knocking on a friend's door when my mother coming in from shopping shouted get away from that house, you know that you are not allowed to play with him.

Pets

I loved my cat Blackie he was a Persian cat and would be a house cat nowadays but was then free to roam. We had a few pets when I was a child, a black and white mongrel called champ that also roamed the streets and would meet me from school but he was taken to the vet to be put down as he bit a council building worker.

We also had a young kitten called Minty and it had fleas and would fight with one of the neighbours kittens called Jinx. They were from the same litter but each morning when let out they would attack each other whilst the neighbours whooped at what basically was cruel sports.

My cat Blackie though was my favourite, he would knock on the letter box situated at the bottom of the door to be let in. If it were the early hours my mother would drag me out of bed 'let that sodden cat in'

Blackie would follow me to bed and settle down at the side of my head with my three teddies, big ted that had no arms, Old faithfull that had the stuffing falling out of it and Sooty, nothing like the children's Sooty but so named all the same.

If Blackie came home when my mother was up she would let him in and he would jump on my bed and place his teeth lightly on my cheek waking me then after the patting routine he would go asleep and still be there in the morning.

One night he never came home and I would rush home from school every day hoping he would be there, I would pray for God to bring him home and spend hours rattling his saucer in the back garden whilst calling his name.

I eventually accepted he was not coming home and it may have been weeks, months even when I was asleep in bed but awoken by what were light footsteps on my bed and stopping by my head. I dare not open my eyes and this unexplainable happening continued over a few more nights.

I believed it was my cat Blackie so why should I be afraid but I was and prayed to God for it to stop it and so it did.

It was not my imagination and I have had a couple of paranormal experiences over my life but non-as vivid as those as a child.

We also had a tortoise which nearly everyone did and you would paint your house number on its shell should it get lost and goldfish that survived about a week in their round glass prison.

When I was a teenager we got a long-haired German shepherd dog we called Rebel. It looked like a wolf was huge and frightened the life out of anyone coming the door. We also had another cat called Whiskers that would follow us meowing whenever we took Rebel for a walk around the block, Whiskers keeping to the safety of the front gardens.

Christmas

Though meant to be a time of joy and happiness Christmas day seldom ended without there being a row between my parents. My father would always arrive late home from his Christmas day drink with his brothers and the dinner would be ruined so we seldom sat down as a family. On the occasions that we did sit down as a family we would be served turkey breast and a wing, carrot and turnip and sprouts none of which I could eat but do enjoy now. I think my mother's cooking left a lot to be desired.

Occasionally we would have Christmas pudding which might have a three-penny bit but never a sixpence in it, once it had a farthing in it.

We would get the annual selection box but could only select from what was left after my parents choose their favourites and that would be repeated at Easter. There would be nothing down for a chocolate father Christmas you would be lucky to have the lower half to eat.

Prior to Christmas dinner my sister and I would watch the Christmas day film which was usually one of Tom Browns school days, Oliver Twist with Bill Sykes or Scrooge with Alastair Sim our favourite Christmas film.

Occasionally in the weeks leading up to Christmas a film would be put on in a local school by Mr Faye and you would get to see Bambi or Snow White.

There was the occasional Christmas Pantomine with Jimmy Tarbuck and Frankie Vaughan and of course the grotto.

I did like the days leading up to Christmas in primary school where we would draw Christmas trees on large flip chart paper then cut them out and paint them to display along with the Christmas chain decorations.

Then there was the grotto were occasionally you would bump into someone from your class. Whenever a pupil was off school for a day leading up to Christmas it would undoubtedly be to go the grotto. Every time they came back to school the class would erupt with 'you went the grotto' 'No I never' and everyone would laugh, even though they all went.

I would gaze in wonder at the silver Christmas trees with pink baubles in the big stores. We had a small green tree more of a sapling covered in bits of tinsel and chocolate decorations that you were not allowed to eat till after Christmas but they miraculously disappeared each day and not at mine or Mary's hands.

My grandad always had a real Christmas tree in King avenue that I would go to Moss Lane with him to pick, I so I loved the smell of a real tree.

We would go carol singing and my friend Ken would be out in front singing 'the holly and the ivy' and he was quite good so we always got money. I remember when I was first elected as councillor there was a family that would send their children out on the pretense that they were carol singing but they would steal wreaths from doors and try and sell them locally. They eventually progressed to stealing garden ornaments and breaking into sheds then houses and all went through the criminal justice system.

I once answered a request in the Liverpool Echo for memories of the grotto as a child and I wrote in as a councillor and how I remembered the dancing waters at Lewis grotto and Blacklers which had a monkey and a small chimp you had your photo taken with and you always got a torch with four colours as a present.

I was working for J Keith Park Solicitors in Walton Vale at the time and over the course of the next few months I would receive a Lewis bag through the post and note saying hello councillor Brennan do you remember me I'm the dancing waters but I have run dry.

Then a picture of a chimpanzee again Hello councillor Brennan do you remember me I'm the chimp but now I'm fully grown then a torch of different colours arrived, hello councillor Brennan I'm the torch with four colours. I never found out the sender's identity but I swear it were a solicitor Nigel who I worked with as one was posted from Hull where he lived the other two from different parts of the country.

I seldom received the presents that I asked for though one year my mother got me a Matchbox garage and as a teenager a Ben Sherman shirt but she was working herself then but mostly I did not get what I asked for.

We were in the city centre or Town as we called it and I pointed at an Action man dressed in an artic snow suit with skis and asked for that for Christmas.

Santa brought me the snow suit and skis but bizarrely forgot the Action man.

Never mind though my grandad bought me a cowboy called Johnny West along with an Indian and stallion with everything including branding irons and quivers it was unbelievable and it became the only cowboy to be dressed in an artic snow suit.

I never did ever get an Action man but was once bought a similar figure called Tommy Gunn though it was not the same when everyone else had an Action man

I never had a Meccano or scale electric or Hornby train set, never owned a kite or fishing rod. It was always the same

'you will have wait to see what Father Christmas brings you'

I swear that Santa forgot to pack all our presents because we were always left disappointed apart from the terrific presents that my grandad would bring us.

My father once took us to the Jacobs Christmas party for the staff children, dropped us in the reception area and we would not see him till the end of the day leaving me and my sister to walk around holding each other's hands all day totally lost.

Over Christmas we would go to my grandads and later grandad and Junes and there would be Brazil nuts, Walnuts and tangerines and Old Oak ham and red salmon and cucumber butties such a feast.

Boxing day blues

Boxing day was always spent at my paternal grandparents in Grieve road Fazakerley an annual event that I looked forward to on equal par with a visit to the dentist. Talking of which I once had eight teeth removed in one go by 'Baker' the dentist who was infamously known as the butcher. I can smell the rubber mask as it was forced onto my face, struggling hard against it and the sickening smell with colours flashing in my eyes then I awoke. I remember going into the dentist in Great Mersey Street which I misread as Mercy Street.

Back to boxing day it all began with the bus to warbreck Moor, the wait outside the Black Bull pub for the bus that took us to Fazakerley, exiting the bus at the Copplehouse pub now an Aldi supermarket. It spelt for me the start of a day that could not pass quickly enough.

We would enter the house and be met by the memorial on the wall and a roaring coal fire that Mick the cat was laying asleep in front of, oblivious to the goings on in the room.

My auntie Betty and uncle Brian would already be there with our cousins Kenneth who was older than me and Janet slightly younger. My auntie Ann and uncle Bill and our cousin Stephen would arrive later and almost immediately all the men except for my grandfather would all depart to the Copplehouse pub.

My grandmother would usher us children into the back garden to do whatever we were supposed to do, be out the way being the main while our grandfather would be sat watching the horse racing.

Eventually we would be called in when it was time for tea then the men would return have their food a few more drinks and then we would thankfully depart for home.

'Yes, thank you god I survived another day at that house'

Once off the bus me and my sister Mary would play a game of who could spot the most Christmas trees in the windows. My mother always appeared quiet and reserved on the visits and I overheard her telling my father that she felt as if his sisters were looking down on her because they were better off than us.

My father was very close to my aunt Ann and uncle Bill and we would regularly go to their house in the Old Roan and we would enjoy days out to New Brighton.

We went for dinner and having had no lunch I did not have to wait for the magical words 'come on tuck in I dove into the plate of corned beef and piccalilli sandwiches.

My aunt went out to fetch in trifle and my mother came around and prodded me saying 'stop making a holy show you think you have had nothing to eat'

'I haven't I replied' to be given an icy stare and finger pointing menacingly at me and the words 'just you wait'

My sister Mary looked across at me and then returned to her sandwich, my cousin Stephen just looked and stared. Shortly afterwards my aunt came in carrying a bowl of trifle that she dished out in equal shares.

I should add that my father and uncle Bill had gone to the Old Roan pub

After we had all eaten there was still about two small dishes full of trifle left

'Come on you three there is more trifle left, Bobby would you like some more?'

I caught my mother's 'don't you bloody say yes' expression but I answered

'Yes, please auntie Ann'

I may as well be hanged for a sheep as for a lamb.

Needless to say, I was punished for my insolence on getting home.

Tragically my cousin Stephen was killed when he was six or seven when he was hit by a vehicle when running out for an ice cream and my aunt could never accept why it was Stephen and not me that was taken.

We were not allowed to go to my paternal grandparents if my auntie Ann was going to be there.

I remember once being there and auntie Ann turned up unannounced and my grandmother came in saying to my father 'you will have to go our Ann is here, go out the back door and through the entry' which we did.

I think that happened on two occasions and we ceased to go again which was great news for me.

The green shed

I mentioned earlier in the book that I would return to the green shed though it is not worth a chapter by itself. One Saturday my father called to Grieve Road as his brother Tom was home from sea and my mother refused to go but my father insisted to my dismay that me and Mary were going as uncle Tom would like to see us.

Whether or not he did was unclear but he gave us half a crown each that my father took for safe keeping never to be seen again despite requests

'Can we have our money please dad'

'What do you need it for the shops are closed'

After they left for the pub I grew bored of stroking Mick the cat and listening to Grandstand and the horse racing. I said to Mary look and pointed at my grandfather's trilbi hat that was placed at the side of the hearth, he had gone upstairs for a minute.

I placed the hat on my head then putting my fist inside it pushed upwards and that once proud trilbi now resembled a bowler hat.

Mary was giggling away as I desperately tried to reshape it when my grandfather came back in and roared 'you little bastard what have you done' His swearing and menacing look frightened me and I started crying at which my grandmother rushed in from the kitchen and said

'What on earth is going on?'

'Look what the little Bastard has done to my Sunday best' came his reply

My grandmother not concerned for my tears said

'You wait till our Bob your father comes back 'at which point my grandfather grabbed me by the ear and frog marched me out into the back garden unbolted the green shed door and pushed me inside.

'Get in there you little bastard' and then he fastened the bolt.

I do not how long I was in that shed for but I found a corner to sit down in and when I needed to pee I would go in the corner of the shed which was all rotted away so my pee was going outside. It was now dusk and back door opened allowing light to shine into the yard. Was I going to be released from my prison the green shed.

My father opened the door and I could smell the alcohol on his breath as he muttered 'you wait till you get home' then he cuffed me around the head.

My grandfather stood at the door shouting 'that little Bastard deserves a good hiding I should have taken my belt to him'. The time I had spent in the shed had not suppressed his anger.

My father replied that he will deal with me and of course the inevitable happened when we got home, I was sent for the belt and then bed.

I had nothing to eat or drink since leaving home that morning and it was now gone nine o'clock at night.

My paternal grandfather had a look of Rudolph Hess with deep set eyes and was by all accounts a bruiser in his younger days. Later in life he developed psychosis and spent time on ward 30 in Fazakerley hospital once covering all the windows in newspaper so no one could look in despite it being the top floor. I was told that he regularly beat his children more so his boys and would turn the picture of the sacred heart around to face the wall before doing so.

There had been one occasion before the green shed which I can barely recall. My nana was in hospital and close to passing and as my father was working shifts in Jacobs we had to stay in Grieve Road for two nights. I remember just wishing for my father to come and collect us, the two days seemed like an eternity and one of horse racing and Mick the cat and little else.

There is no further that I can add regarding my paternal grandparents. When my grandmother died my grandfather came to stay at our house in Simons Croft and I was ejected from my bedroom for about a week. I remember going back in after he left and my room smelt of tobacco smoke and the bed sheets were not washed so I lay on top of the bed for a few days till my mother took the sheets to the launderette. I recall my mother had to address my grandfather as Mr Brennan and she always called my grandmother Mrs Brennan.

When my grandfather passed away I was seventeen and my father went to the funeral alone and told his siblings that he had forbade me to attend which was fine by me I would not mourn his passing.

My father had a younger sister called Mary who emigrated to the United States and lived in Long island.

I see her only a few times as a child but eventually she returned to the UK and met and married my uncle Peter Raymond Saunders who my father never liked for whatever reason.

Peter was a painter and decorator and a wonderful uncle and remained close to my own family till he passed away in early 2023, my auntie Mary died several years earlier from cancer.

My father's other brothers Tom and Tony have both passed on.

Tom was attacked by about three or four men in 1999 whilst cutting through an underpass on his way home from the British legion club in Blackpool.

He was robbed of his wallet and Rolex which was later found in a jeweler in London leading to the arrest of the assailants who were all convicted of manslaughter.

Tom having made it home after the attack but died of the head injuries he received shortly afterwards.

Tony the youngest brother passed away in June 2024 of cancer just a few weeks before my mother passed away. No one knew Tony had cancer he was a very private individual.

My cousin Kenneth passed away a few years ago and I'm the sole surviving male grandchild of the Brennan family.

I hope they are all happy at peace and re-united with John

Days out in Ford

As boys we would make our own entertainment, which would be bike rides afar as long as an older sensible boy was with us.

We would cycle to Formby to search for newts in the ponds that we would catch and return.

I never had a bike so would borrow my friends' sisters' bike, no crossbar but it had two wheels and allowed for me to participate in the bike rides.

We would walk to Litherland park with its giant slide and witch's hat, buying cinder toffee on the way from a small shop in Sefton road.

The occasional trip to the Broadway stores opposite the Bootle Odeon, were we would buy caps for a cap gun if you were lucky to have one or a catapult, followed by a walk-up Stanley Road to North park to see the floral clock that was made out of spring and summer flowers

For some reason we never ventured into North park or Derby park to play, Litherland park being the only park we would visit, though we once went to Potters barn in Waterloo searching for birds' eggs.

I would accompany my friends to the Wizards den in the city centre where they would buy stink bombs to let off in school and the dreaded itching powder that I was unfortunate to once have tipped down my shirt collar by one troublesome Holy Ghost pupil who also singed the back of my hair with a match one night in the cubs, happily his family emigrated to Australia.

On one occasion we were cycling home from Formby and were stopped by Lancashire constabulary enquiring if we were the owners of the bikes as one had been stolen in Formby by boys with Liverpool accents.

'Right you lot what have you been up to?'

'We have been to Formby Sir and going home '

'And where is home?'

'Ford sir'

'And where is Ford when it is at home?'

'It is in Bootle' we replied   puzzled that the officer had not heard of it.

'Bootle, I might have known, are these your bikes?'

'Yes, I replied along with the others to which my friend said 'it is not yours'

'Well if it is not yours who does it belong to?' 'It is his sisters' bike I said'

'Okay names and addresses'

After a short delay the officer returned to us and said 'right on your way and don't let me see you out this way again'

Crosby baths was always a trip we undertook a couple of times during school holidays and I would attend if I had the money. One time after leaving the baths we were going for the train home and I noticed a clump of daffodils in the garden of a large derelict house that I went and picked for my mum.

As we walked onto the platform we were halted by a shout and turned around to see the man from the ticket office pointing at the daffodils.

'Where did you get them from I bet you stole them?'

47

'I never I picked them from the garden of an empty house for my mum'

'Don't give me that clap trap, all you lot do is come here and steal and damage property, leave them on that bench and If I see you around here again you will feel the weight of my boot on your backside'

Leaving the daffodils on the bench we waited on the platform for the train and watched as the bunch of daffodils were taken into the ticket office and we boarded the train having once again been subject to false accusations and bias.

We would walk to Sefton village and explore the graveyard at St Helens church then cross the road a little way past the Punch Bowl pub where you can find the site of St Helens well.

There used to be dairy cows in the field opposite the Punch Bowl and a path just afterwards on the right that was made of crushed sea shells that we would walk down till it came to reed beds and the river Alt.

There was a small shop at Sefton mill that sold homemade lemonade which we would buy and share. In fact, we shared everything even apples that we would each take a bite of.

On other days we would get an old milk crate and rope and dredge the pond in Bootle golf course, dredging lots of golf balls that we would then clean and sell back to the golfers at the club house.

We would also dredge what appeared to be oyster or mussel shells up and toss them back in but I never got to identify what exactly they were. Golfers would haggle with us but we always insisted on at least a three-penny bit per golf ball. Often our expedition was thwarted by the cocky watchman on the golf course and we would retreat to the safety of the field on Boundary lane till it was safe to return to the dredge. We would often hear a shouted warning and duck down as golf balls whistled over our heads some landing in the pond.

Not all golfers welcomed our presence and many told us to 'get the fuck off their' followed by more expletives.

Sometimes the miscreants would set fire to the field and smoke would engulf Boundary lane and the golf course till the fire brigade arrived so it was no wonder we were not universally welcome being tarred with the same brush.

There would be street outings to Frith beach, Rhyl and my favourite Belle-Vue amusement park in Manchester that had a zoo and a fun fair and one of the best model villages you could ever see. The school would also have the annual day trip to Llangollen for the Eisteddfod festival for those about to leave the school. I was not that keen on the festival but just going to Wales was fantastic. We would cheer as we entered the Mersey tunnel on leaving Liverpool and cheer as we came back out the tunnel at the end of the day because we were back home again.

We went to Trentham Gardens twice but it was on a coach trip arranged through a woman my mother knew. I had no friends going and found the whole day boring and though I would eventually like gardening I was not yet at that age to appreciate Rhododendrons in bloom. I did though collect a bag full of conkers they were everywhere but I soon lost them all in the Conker fights with one boy in the street having a vinegar hardened Goliath of a Conker.

We never went on any of the street outings to Frith beach or Rhyl as my mother was not interested and I would stare out my bedroom window as the coach boarded and departed and imagined being on it. My mother never minded Belle-Vue as her so called best friend and her children always went.

I had started to save money from my paper round and at least I could afford to go on some of the rides though needed to spread the rides out throughout the day.

There were two exhilarating attractions the Bobs which was believed to be the largest rollercoaster in Europe and assumed to be so named as it cost a shilling 'bob' to go on it and the smaller scenic railway that was still nerve wracking.

Not having enough money to purchase a hot dog or burger I would have to await my mother going to the restaurant later in the day.

My mother would order a plate of chips each and being hungry I poured what I believed was salt on my chips and realised to my horror it was sugar in the glass container.

'You can just get them ate, you are getting nothing else'

Reluctantly I ate sweetened chips for the first and last time.

Two of my friends that lived in a neighbouring street had paid to come on the street outing as there was always places spare and they each took a couple of figures from the model railway a sheep dog and something else but were seen and apprehended and dragged to the coach.

My mother pointed the finger at me 'they are your friends it is your bloody fault' of course no harm was done the figures were returned to their places but it was seemingly my fault albeit I was on the coach when they sneaked back to take the figures home as presents for their mothers.

Blackpool lights

Every year the street would go to Blackpool to see the lights and have about two hours to spend in Blackpool before boarding the coach again and the drive through the promenade lights before heading home. Unfortunately, all the boys would go off together but I had to stay with my mother and sisters.

'Take that look of your face, you are not going off with them'

Probably just as well as I had no money to spend on the fair or anything else for that matter.

Oh, how I hated the laughing clown, he had no sympathy for my plight

Paper round

When I was 14 I got a paper round that I loved and I would have to give my sisters pocket money from it and of course allow Mary to read the Bunty comic before it was delivered.

'Mum I have to deliver the comic I'm going to be late'

'You can wait till Mary has finished her comic'

'But it is not Mary's comic'

'Anymore out of you and you will not have a paper round'

Off I would go delivering the papers, knowing that as soon as I got a couple of doors away someone would shout 'hey there is no comic'

'Sorry I may have left it in the other sack'

On one occasion getting back home to retrieve the comic I gasped in disbelief as the cut-out costumes on the back page of the Bunty were laying on the floor having literally been cut out.

'Mum, Mary has cut the comic I cannot deliver that now'

It was never delivered and I had to pay for the missing comic out of my paper round money.

My sister had me expelled from the mobile library a few years earlier.

I could take out three books and was really excited about going to the mobile library that was in Simons croft once per week.

My mother said 'you can get Mary a book' you won't want three books.

I took out three books, two books for me and reluctantly one for Mary, a ladybird book titled

'The story of Ned the lonely donkey'

I read through that book on the walk home along the street.

A week later I returned the books to the library and was browsing through the children's section when the librarian grabbed my shoulder and said

'Is this how you treat library books, well you are not getting any more from here' I gasped in horror as on nearly every page the words poo was written in green pen

Having been ordered off the library bus I tearfully walked home and told my mother I was not allowed in the library again because Mary had written poo in the book. My mother's sole response was

'Well you will just have to make do with your comic'

Easter

I never cared much for Easter and the school processions that we had rehearsed for weeks. We would get one Easter egg each usually a Smarties that we would have to leave on top of the sideboard alongside the chocolate rabbit with miniature eggs and decorated in little yellow chicks that my grandad would buy us and an occasional egg from an auntie or my mother's friend.

'Mum can I open an Easter egg?' 'offer your father some first' and as very much expected my father would take half of the egg 'you don't mind me having half, do you?' Then it was my mother's turn and so I would be left with just a quarter of the egg. Once my grandad bought me a milk tray Easter egg and after my father took his half my mother took the small bag of sweets leaving me with half an egg that I had to eat over the next two days.

How I hated my friends in the square who would walk out with half an egg and devour it and later return with another half.

Salvation Army

The Sally army would always come into the square each Christmas to sing and play carols and it was always a nice occasion but my mother would never have any money to give to the collection. Once one of the families that were members of the Sally army arranged a football match on the Orrell pleasures now the site of the Army reserve centre and the former Girobank.

The Orrell pleasures pitches were infamously known for being flooded and none more so than on the occasion of this match. We turned up and there were about fifty lads from the estate all seeking to play in the game that kicked off with everyone chasing the ball there being no sides picked. It resembled Tom Browns school days and the football game at Rugby school. There was mud flying, crunching tackles and as we were all in different kits no one knew who was on what side, needless to say, that was the first and last Salvation army match.

My father once came up with the idea of starting a football team and had me sending out messages far and wide for players all of whom would turn up at our house in Simons Croft to be interviewed.

Of course, no team was ever formed and It was just another embarrassing episode for me.

My father claimed to have jointly held the Zingari football league record for most goals scored but whether this was true I never got to find out but he did play amateur football and I do remember seeing him play once on fields in Lower lane in Fazakerley.

For information the name Zingari means 'the gypsies' in dialecticisied Italian.

My uncle Tony my father's youngest brother confirmed that my dad did play amateur football but also told me that my father was 'a very jealous man' and 'never liked people getting on' and though in my late twenties I made my piece with him his behaviour at times did still cause me to question why I still put up with him.

My parents are not here to defend themselves but If I'm to tell the story of my childhood with its hardship and punishment meted out I cannot paint over aspects of that life and have to tell it warts and all.

My father was considered to be an extremely handsome man with dark hair and brown eyes and had the look of Hollywood heart throb James Gardner. He had several affairs that impacted greatly on my life and that of my mother who stood by him all of her married life even though she knew of some if not all of his extra marital relationships.

One embarrassing event being their silver wedding anniversary that was held in a club in Skelmersdale that he failed to attend, making the excuse that he could not leave the factory in Brighton where he was a personnel officer claiming that the IRA had given a bomb warning.

The alleged bomb threat was not reported in any media and only believed by my mother.

My mother's so-called best friend who had been conducting a long running affair with my father through the 1960s and early 1970s did turn up with her husband and of course could not contain her amusement.

If my mother ever knew of that relationship she never believed it as they remained friends and she would confide in this woman about my father wanting a divorce.

My father would boast about his conquests and the relationship he had with that woman and others.

He claimed to feel sorry for the hurting spouse but unsurprisingly never expressed any for my mother.

However, the embarrassment of her husband not being at the silver wedding anniversary should have been enough for my mother but her main concern on the night was that I did not tell people I was 25 years old.

That instruction was not well received by me, I mean what the hell, why add to the madness and conceal the truth.

I was also ordered to watch who my youngest sister was with, so I got two sausage rolls placed them before my eyes like binoculars and informed my sister I had her under surveillance, what complete nonsense.

Back to Ford

I never had ice creams when the van came around apart from odd occasions when Jack our next door neighbour who lived in the ground floor flat was home from sea. Jack got on well with my father him being an ex-merchant seaman and my mother would look after Jacks flat.

Jack always appeared drunk and would buy all the kids in the square a Walls ice cream.

He would also bring me home several National Geographic magazines taking me to a world I never knew.

Jack once brought me a model of the Japanese battleship the Yamato as I had started collecting airfix models that I would build and paint and hang from my bedroom ceiling, German Dornier bomber, Lancaster bomber and spitfire and Hurricane and Japanese Zero.

Sadly, Jack fell into the dock in Bootle and drowned and it was assumed that he was intoxicated.

As kids we would do the usual pranks, Knick knock on doors and run away and I was always singled out
'It was a little lad with black hair'
'Oh, that will be Bobby Brennan'

My friend Kens back garden backed onto the garden of a house in Hampshire avenue of a Jehovah Witness family.

One Sunday one of the boys was playing on the garden swing prior to going off to their place of worship. He was wearing the crispest white shirt I had ever seen. Kens father had blackcurrant bushes and every time the boy swung backwards he was in range of the blackcurrants that pelted his back reducing the once crisp white shirt to one of a polka dot shirt. We heard him being called to go and then the cries of anguish on seeing his shirt and we dived for cover behind the blackcurrant bushes as the rest of the family arrived at the fence peering through to see who the culprits were.

Camping out

Camping out was another pastime enjoyed during the summer holidays and we would camp out in each other's gardens or on the field at Boundary lane. Camping enabled us to plunder birds' nests in gardens that were otherwise inaccessible during the day and our raiding party would spring into action at the crack of dawn.

We would also leave notes in the empty milk bottles for a carton of orange juice or one extra pint and sneak back and collect the extra pint or carton and sometimes we left notes saying no milk today thanks.

Camping out in late Autumn was always timed to coincide with apples being ready and we would strip the tree and also carry out raids on other streets bonfires that we would set ablaze then we would disappear into the night as the flames lit up the surrounding houses.

We only put our bonfire together on 05 November so as to prevent ours being destroyed. Scurrying back and forth with mattresses, wood, trees all of which had been stored in back gardens and even on top of the electric substation in Simons Croft and our bommie would up and ready within an hour.

We would watch each neighbour light their fireworks with ours always being the cheapest box of Standard fireworks or sometimes Paine's with a couple of traffic lights and a Mount Vesuvius which was more of a hillock by its performance and sparklers, never any rockets or Catherine wheels for us.

Coronation park Boating lake

We would walk to Coronation park boating lake in Crosby to sail our boats, well my friends all had yachts and I had a tin clockwork liner with light up port and starboard lights. We would walk past what was known as Bluebell wood albeit there was very few trees and no bluebells, then down through froggy meadow and onto the boating lake.

Everyone had heard of froggy meadow it was the place to get tadpoles and of course frogs.

On arriving at the boating lake, you would be met by signs saying no hydroplanes and strictly no getting into the lake which was really not an option as the lake was full of broken bottles.

In went the yachts sailing gracefully around the lake and in went the clockwork liner wound up to go the shorter distance across the lake. So pleased was I to see it chugging away making its way to the other side but my pleasure turned to anguish as it suddenly stopped rolled on its side and sank, its rusted hull likely still there today.

My friends all fell about with laughter as did others watching the spectacle.

'It's the Titanic someone shouted' oh shit I thought how do I explain this away and I could not wade in salvage it.

I arrived home a few hours later to tell my mother the news and blurted out

'My boat sank'

'What do you mean, your boat sank, where is it?'

'It sank in the lake'

'Bloody stupid little bugger your uncle Tony bought you that you should have just played with it in the bath'

I was grounded and retired to my bedroom to watch my friends coming out to play after their tea and I stayed in my room till the following morning when it was time to go to Sunday mass.

One time at the boating lake a man on a bike shouted 'look out for the sharks; which we mimicked. He followed us all the way up the path through froggy meadow lashing out at us with a stick forcing us to run into the reed beds where we continued to shout 'look out for the sharks'

Halloween & Duck apple

It is not like today there was no dressing up as ghouls or pumpkins you were grateful to have a turnip you could carve a face in and there was no mischief night. If my father was home he would lift us over the sink and we would try to bite the apple but always got water in our noses and he put chestnuts on the griddle that would burst open the shells shooting off in every direction sending the cat screaming out the kitchen. My mother on the other hand would sit me and Mary in the bath and once when the two apples were about to be tossed in I seen a stream of yellow and shouted 'Mum Mary has weed in the bath' too late the apples hit the bath water with a splash.

I dived out shouting 'I'm not getting back in there or eating them apples now'.

My mother instead of being understanding whacked me around the head and sent me to bed. 'Well you will not have any then' So, there I was in my room listening to my sister chomping on not one but two apples.

Things were not all that bad, the mother of one of my friends would make toffee apples at Halloween which were delicious and the only times I got to eat one.

Holidays

The first holiday with my mother and father was in the early sixties to a boarding house in Llandudno. It rained every day we were on holiday and we spent every day in the arcades while my Father played the fruit machines that had pictures of pop stars on them such as Helen Shapiro, Connie Francis and Cilla Black, occasionally we could go on the penny push. I think we made one trip up the Great Orme on the railway but again it was raining.

Coming home from that holiday my parents were fighting over whatever and I took myself off to my room and played with my cowboys and Indians. I would adopt one of the cowboy figures and ride out with John Wayne into the plains and the Rockies to do battle with the Indians blissfully ignorant to the commotion downstairs.

Nearly everyone in the square apart from us went to Butlins in Pwllheli for two weeks with one family of five children crowded into Minor 1000 station wagon.

We were promised a Pontins holiday but that never happened.

Our next holiday and the start of a few years great memories was to Port St Mary in the Isle of Man in 1966 just after the world cup final when we stayed in the large house of a friend of my step nan June.

Walking up the gang plank onto the steam packet ship was exciting but the four-hour trip always ended with us being sea sick particularly if it was a rough crossing.

Gannett's flying around the ship seemed to indicate we were getting close and then the island came into view and we sailed into Douglas harbour past the Tower of Refuge. I recall the names of those steam ships, the Manx Man, Manx Maid, Ben-My- Chree and Monas Isle.

My wife had an uncle who was a seaman and worked the IOM ferries and left his belongings on the Ben- My- Chree and went overboard in 1972, his body was never found but it is believed he had been diagnosed with cancer.

We would visit Peel castle and castle Rushen in Castletown, Port Erin and my favourite place of all time Perwick bay not far from Port St Mary golf course.

There used to be a hotel the Perwick bay hotel that stood at the top of the cliffs and an open-air swimming pool that Sarah who later married Mike Pilling would give us swimming lessons.

Perwick bay was great for exploring the rock pools and I would find large scallop shells that would be used for ash trays and Robert Pilling once caught an eel that was taken back and cooked.

That bay holds for me my sweetest childhood memory with the bay ablaze with orange Crocosmia plants bulbs some of which I pulled out for my grandad.

There was a football pitch at the rear of the house we were staying in Port St Mary and I would climb on the wall and watch Jackdaws going about their business. One evening a young girl and a boy that lived on the island came over and we played for about an hour on the field. The girl suggested we play catch the girl kiss the girl and would allow me to catch her straight away every time much to the other boy's annoyance.

The romantic interlude was briefly interrupted by an older boy another holiday maker and a bully by all accounts. He came over and pushed me in order to impress the young girl's older sister who had appeared saying 'If you want to kiss me then punch him' Grinning like a Cheshire cat he rolled up his sleeves he said 'It will be my absolute pleasure'

Now given my not being bothered about size I landed a punch on his nose before he could raise his fist and he ran off crying never to appear again.

The girl's older sister tutted and walked away whilst my two new friends cheered and our game resumed.

I took my two youngest children to the IOM on the sea cat and on a very rainy afternoon we walked across the cliff tops to Perwick bay and down the path to the bay with its Crocosmia bulbs in full bloom. The path down seemed less steep and a lot shorter than when I was a child.

My children climbed onto a large rock that me and my sister Mary has similarly climbed up on and a photograph taken of us. As they stood on that rock a tear rolled down my cheek, it was as if time itself had stood still. I could see my grandad and June and hear the summer sounds of the sixties from June's Bush radio.

I once again gathered some Crocosmia bulbs turned and looked down the bay it seemed I was destined to see the bay one last time in my life. If it were possible to go back in the past just for one day I would go there.

My second favourite place on the IOM was the witches mill and Rushen Abbey and the Silverburn river and glen. I loved to explore catching sight of the perch in the water and numerous Mallard ducklings that I once tried to catch but whatever I would have done with one I do not know.

After a few glorious and memorable years my father decided we were no longer holidaying in Port St Mary with my grandad and June and we started to stay in a boarding house on the promenade in Douglas. The proprietor had a teenage son who had severe learning difficulties who would run up and down the stairs shouting obscenities and had to repeatedly apologise to guests and continued unabated for the duration of the holiday. The first time we stayed in that boarding house I was in secondary school and had to wear my St Thomas Aquinas school blazer as part of my holiday clothes and though we did go to Perwick bay those holidays were never the same without my grandad and June.

My parents met a nice older couple who lived in Dingle and they introduced us to Port Soderick where there were ammonite fossils in the rocks. I was recently looking at images of Port Soderick and there is now nothing there, it is unrecognizable from its 1960s hey days.

The dreaded eleven plus
I had not passed the eleven plus and recall the look of revulsion on my mother's face when the letter arrived from Lancashire education authority delivering the news that I was a failure. The fact that only one boy in the square passed and her close friends' children also failed did not matter a jot but for me I was delighted as all my best friends failed and where going to St Thomas Aquinas secondary modern with me. The failure though meant no bragging rights for my mother, well not for four years till I passed the entrance exam to go to Bootle Technical college when at last she could parade the pass letter to the neighbours whose sons had failed the entrance exam.

The Cinema
I enjoyed going to the cinema or the pictures as we would call them and my mother took us to see The Beatles 'Hard day's night' at the Carlton in Orrell park and the Beatles 'Help' at the Bootle Odeon. On both occasions we went with my mother's friend and her children, though she was more of a friend to my father if you get the picture, no pun intended.

Many years later I and a friend went to see 'Kelly's Heroes' one of the last films shown at the Carlton which opened on 01 September 1930 and closed its doors on 02 February 1974.

We also went to see one of the last films at the Bootle Odeon 'That'll be the day' which closed on 01 November 1975. It was first opened as The Broadway and was destroyed by German bombs on 08 May 1941.

The shop The Broadway stores opposite the old Bootle Odeon owned by the Armstrong family since it opened its doors in 1927 remained open during the May blitz.

As a family we went to see the Alamo which was showing on I think was the Gaumont and once my father took me to see 'The Magnificent Seven' on the Bootle Odeon. I remember being in my last year of Holy Ghost primary and he had promised to take me to see 'The Bridge over the river Kwai' I did nothing but talk about it all day in class and ran home rather than walk with my friends but any joy was short lived as on arriving home I was told we would not be going as my dad had no money.

My mother would drag me along to see the musicals of the day 'The sound of music' and the box office failure 'Paint your wagon' I had no interest whatsoever in those films and had to sit through Lee Marvin drawl

'I was born under a wandering star'

He was though a great war movie actor and had served in the Pacific campaign with the USMC.

I saved my paper round money to go and see a couple of films 'The Battle of Britain' and also 'Zulu' which we were nearly ejected from as we could not contain ourselves with the opening scenes as bare breasted Zulu women were being married off to warriors. We were repeatedly told to behave by those in front and behind us and having received a stern warning by the usher we settled down to watch the film in silence.

The children's Saturday show at the Bootle was a sight to behold and not one for the faint hearted. It was total chaos and fighting always broke out. I went once and never again as you could not sit and watch anything. I think it was about halfway through 'Champion the wonder horse' when I was being fisted in the back of head causing the usual retaliatory behaviour.

Other memories

Notwithstanding the big freeze of 1963 and burst boilers most of my childhood winters were cold with frequent snowfall. We would make a snowman in our front gardens and some were really good with coal for buttons, carrot nose and hat and scarves. Alas not mine and my sisters we would use stones for the eyes and placed a Liverpool bobble hat on it. I recall it was always foggy even into the early 1970s and you could not see beyond a couple of metres with ships on the Mersey sounding their fog horns. There was a lot of shipping on the docks at that time with ships waiting at the bar for their turn to dock and be unloaded. Some ships would be in dock for a few days not like the quick turnaround of today and you had neighbours that worked on the docks.

As children going to get the bus to my grandads in King avenue we would always be excited to see a statue in the front garden of a house in Appleby drive that we believed was 'Humpty Dumpty' but was in fact a stone buddha.

61

Then one day in 1972 whilst delivering papers It had been destroyed, its head broken off and in pieces. I remember being shocked at this act of wanton vandalism and a sign of in Bob Dylan's words

'The times, the times they are changing'.

The Co-op store in the Marian square Netherton went on fire once and all the smoke damaged tins were being sold off at only a few pence and my mother dragged me up and down to the supermarket to queue up and bring back tins of beans and spaghetti and we must have made the journey from Simons Croft to the Marian square about three times one afternoon.

Harvest festival

Harvest festival was a time when we would be expected to bring in fruit and vegetables for the poor of the parish. My mother would give us a tin of marrowfat peas or Cross and Blackwell beans never any fresh fruit or vegetables and we were once gifted with a basket of fresh fruit and vegetables to take home being identified as a family in need.

One day I would be supporting vulnerable families in West Lancashire through the Skelmersdale unemployed workers centre where we set up a food co-operative enabling families to receive fresh fruit and vegetables and this before food banks became the norm in society.

Politics

The political climate in the sixties and early seventies was one of central politics with voters turning to Harold Wilson Labour or Ted Heath Conservatism. You would see the vote Labour posters in nearly every window save for the one vote Conservative poster that appeared in the window of the Mormon family that led to them being further considered an oddity.

Local politics in Bootle was dominated by the Mahon family with Simon Mahon the MP. When I started out in my working life as a painter and decorator apprentice my foreman Myles Mahon was the nephew of Simon Mahon.

Myles brother Jimmy was a Bootle and then Sefton councillor and as a plumber worked on the sites. I met Jimmy again after 20 years following my being elected to serve the residents of Orrell ward in 1994.

I served as his deputy chair to the housing committee then later alongside his daughter Sue after she was elected.

When I resigned my seat as a Sefton councillor after 28.6 years Sue was the only councillor that kept in contact with me and periodically enquired about my family's wellbeing.

When I think that I have covered all my early years I remember something that I had missed and recall watching the Russian invasion of Czechoslovakia on the television in a neighbours house. Sitting in the square with other children listening to an older girl's transistor radio and the assassination of senator Bobby Kennedy. I further remember hearing of the assassination of Doctor Martin Luther king and Vietnam which was never off the television. I remember my father directing abuse at the television when there was a stop the war demonstration outside the American embassy in Grosvenor square.

'Lazy long haired good for nothings'

'Lock every one of them up'

Also, his loathing of Muhammed Ali for refusing to fight in Vietnam and always

'Henry Cooper would be the world champion if it weren't for his cut eye'.

My friend Ken of the blackcurrant bushes fame would bring us out bottles of ginger beer that his father made and we would have sugar butties if no jam was available. Me and Ken and another friend who name I cannot recall once walked from Ford to Lydiate to pick blackcurrants. Being paid half a crown for a basket it took hours to fill so we only managed one basket each then set off on the long walk home again. I met up with Ken many years later as he was working in the same building as me in Waterloo, Ken now a social worker.

Ken would occasionally play in our street team and wore rugby boots so would take all the free kicks. Once whilst we were sitting in the square Ken came out and hit a marble with a golf stick sending it right through one of the houses front windows and remarked that he had aimed it the side door of the house.

We also had the local model builder who would purchase airfix models and once assembled and painted would be placed on a small floatable piece of wood on the canal and set on fire like a Viking funeral with no explanation ever given.

63

There were some bizarre characters that lived in Ford, some you would not even consider for a second to play Knick knock on their doors and others that were straight out of a comic book.

One man would grow cabbages in his front garden and hurl abuse at us if we crept in to collect the cabbage white caterpillars that were chomping away on them, even though we were doing him a service.

I remember the mayor paying a fleeting visit to our street party to celebrate the Bootle centenary in 1968 and the opening of the New strand that once had a North End Music Store (NEMS) owned by Beatles manager Brian Epstein

There were two houses in Simons Croft that competed against each other for the best Bootle garden and one of them always won. I think that was the first time I admired hybrid tea rose bushes and honeysuckle.

My doctor was Dr David Flanagan, his practice in Moss Lane Orrell was formerly that of his uncle and had been there since before the second world war. I can still smell the ethanol and see the huge filing cabinet which he would pull out your file and write a few notes then prescribe the medication which you got from the surgery. There is a bottle of chest medicine called BM or black magic that brings back the smell of the doctor's surgery and contains ethanol, chloroform and treacle and still available in a chemist in Liverpool and it guarantees a good night's sleep and I would buy a few bottles for my father in his twilight years.

Before starting in St Thomas Aquinas, I would be sent across from Ford to Daleacre drive shops every Sunday morning get my father The Sunday Mirror, The News of the World and The People and had to run the gauntlet of the gang that frequented the shops.

Similarly, if sent across to the barbers on Daleacre drive you would have to take spare football cards to give to the gang in exchange for your life.

'Hey any football cards to swap?'

'Yes, I have a few'

'What school do you go to'

'Holy Ghost but going to St Thomas Aquinas in September'

'We go there give us your cards and we will protect you' so I handed over the cards in what became a frequent exchange if they were sat outside the shops.

I asked my father why he did not get his papers delivered and he replied 'because I'm not paying a weekly bill' it made no sense whatsoever there was no logic to it but then I suppose there was. My dad would do both Littlewoods and Vernon's pools, the spot the ball and the daily horse racing.

'Where have you been?' get this coupon to the pools lady before it's too late' and I would have to make sure I was around to deliver his coupons to the respective collectors each Friday albeit they both resided less than 100 yards from our house.

The Lottery

When the lottery came out my father would do it on a Wednesday and a Saturday then along came the Euro lottery so he would be compelled to play that also and would never miss a draw fearing his numbers would come upon the one occasion he didn't do the draw.

When my father passed away my mother asked if anyone wanted to continue doing the same numbers.

Unsurprisingly there were no takers to the offer.

I never got on with my father from my early teens until I was about 28 years of age till after he had lost his employment.

From once flying high as a personal officer to be considered too old at 49 then working as a security guard at the Arndale centre then a carer in a nursing home he never really got over the loss of status and higher earnings.

One time when I was in my late twenties I went for a drink with my father to the Horseshoe pub in Old Skelmersdale.

As soon as you entered there was a fruit machine that he just stood and played in between sending me the bar.

He had run out of change so sat down at the table next to the fruit machine and asked me to get a fiver worth of change from the bar.

Whilst at the bar a man came in the pub with a disabled child and put 50p in the machine which hit the jackpot straight away on the first turn.

My father turned to me and said
'forget the change'

Personal hygiene and the nit nurse

I seldom got the luxury of a bath as my mother would tell my sister to leave the water in so I could get in after her which I never did. I would arrive home from working on a building site needing a bath but would instead boil a kettle and get washed at the sink. It was pointless trying to run another bath of hot water as the emersion heater was stone cold.

Once my father complained of my having body odour and my mother scrubbed my neck with a nail brush and vim to get rid of a tide mark. My neck was scrubbed that hard it bled in places and I had to bathe in carbolic soap for weeks. The smell permeating the air around me in class fortunately it was not an uncommon smell.

The nit nurse would be a visitor in primary school but not in secondary school and I sat at home one night aged about 12 scratching my head. My mother having noticed told me to fetch the steel nit comb from the first aid tin and some brown paper which she placed on her lap. Then she dragged the comb through my hair delivering a blow to my head each time a nit case fell on the paper 'your sodden head is lousy' there followed the derbac soap scrubbing of my scalp and the following day I was sent off to the barbers.

I hated going to the barbers because I always had to have a short back and sides or short back and penny arrow bar as we would call it.

My friends were all sporting cropped hair so when I was sat in the barber's chair in Daleacre drive 'right what are we doing for you today'

'crop' I replied and so I got a crop and walked home feeling ever so proud looking like my friends. As soon as the front door was opened by my sister the shout went out 'mum our Bobby has got a skinhead' my mother came rushing in from the kitchen and took one look at the new hairstyle and gave me a whack to the side of the head knocking me onto the couch.

'You wait till your father comes home'

I was grounded for two weeks, only allowed out to deliver my papers and attend school.

Jacobs biscuit tin

When my father worked in Jacobs he would occasionally bring home a tin of broken biscuits including chocolate club and caramel digestives that me and Mary loved. The problem was my mother also liked those biscuits and the tin was kept on the ledge in their room covered by items of folded clothing.

'Mum can we have a biscuit?'

'Go and fetch the tin down' at which she would open the tin and pass us out a biscuit of her choosing.

'Can't we have a club?'

'No, you can have one in the week'

We would return the tin to its place on the bedroom ledge whilst our mother settled down with a cup of coffee and three club biscuits.

One night I waited till the coronation street music came on and crept into my mother's bedroom carefully removing the folded clothing and silently opening the tin lid putting my hand inside to feel for the club biscuits I would gather about four and share them with Mary and creep out the room but the landing floor always creaked.

'Whoever that is get in bed '

'I'm going the toilet mum'

'Get in bed now'

We were able to carry out the commando raids over a couple of nights then one morning.

'Right who has been eating the chocolate biscuits?'

'Not me'

'Nor me'

'Well I have counted them so that will stop you both'

When coronation street came on I decided to launch a further raid which turned out to be the final raid as my mother had indeed counted the biscuits, or at least the chocolate clubs and I would await the belt.

Cadets

I once joined TS Renown sea cadets in Field lane Litherland now TS Starling but only lasted two weeks as I could not afford to pay the subs.

I similarly joined the air cadets in Carr Meadow Hey which being on the estate seemed a lot easier to stay involved in but once my friends drifted away which was not long after joining I also left though I was often late arriving after parade due to my paper round. When I became mayor of Sefton one of our attendants Fred was as former member of that squadron and I knew some of the cadets he mentioned by name. It would be some years before I gave my oath of allegiance to her majesty the queen and all her heirs and successors and proudly put on a uniform.

St Thomas Aquinas

And so, began my first day of the next four years I was in 1X being the top class in the 1st year but ended up in 1T by the end of the year. I guess my being called into the headmistress office in Holy Ghost school was warranted. I stayed in the second class through the next four years but did become captain of St Benedict house football team which was one of four houses, the others being St Bernard, St Dominic and St Francis.

To be given the house captain badge was an achievement but I had already gained the admiration of some of the teaching staff for my prowess on the running track representing the school at cross country, the 1500 metres and 4 x 100 metre relay.

Teachers

I had some of the best and worst teachers in that school, my first-year teacher was Mr Mike Collins who also played for Leigh rugby club.

There were other teachers that played rugby, Mr Shepherd and Mr Chatterton who I think played for Waterloo.

Mr Collins and Mr Myers took PT and I found myself back in a school football team and remained in the team whilst they managed the team.

Alas a new member of the teaching staff then took responsibility for selecting the team and I was booted off for one reason only I showed little interest in his geography class so I was taught a lesson for not learning a lesson.

'Brennan, pay attention' followed by 'where is the Murray Darling basin?'

'It's in Australia sir'

'Yes, we all know that but where about in Australia is it to be found'

'Don't know sir it's a big country'

'It's not a country it's a continent, go and wait outside Mr Griffiths office'

Mr Griffiths being the deputy head would cane you before asking why you were there, the assumption being you had done something wrong.

'Brennan get your hands out of your pockets'

Whack the cane came down on your fingertips, 'next hand'

Whack 'now get back to your lesson'

Outside another unfortunate victim was waiting to enter.

'You boy in'

I stood and listened momentarily to hear the immortal words 'hold your hand out' then the sound of Rattan reed cane meeting flesh.

Blowing air on my smarting fingers I made my way back to my class to be asked the usual daily question

'How many did you get?'

'two' I replied'

'Let's see did it hurt' said another before the words 'quiet in class or you will all be outside Mr Griffiths office'

Thinking back, it was akin to Mathew Modine character private joker in the film Full metal Jacket. 'You write born to kill on your helmet and you wear a peace button, what's that supposed to be some kind of sick joke'

'It is about the duality of war sir' The colonel not amused responds 'get with the programme, or you will find yourself standing tall before the man'

Mr Griffiths would be out on the school field most lunch hours and occasionally after school whacking a golf ball having already appointed some unfortunate to retrieve the balls.

I recall my friend Paul saying 'makes a change from whacking us'

On a happier note I could not be booted off the school athletics team only the football team.

I heard years later that the football teacher had his teacher registration removed due to his conduct towards pupils and upheld complaints.

Stalag Luft

One day one of Mr Griffiths golf shoes was hidden and the reaction was akin to a second world war search for a radio in a German Stalag Luft POW camp.

'Wo betide the boy or boys responsible' and 'no stone will be left unturned'

And so multiple searches were conducted till at last the shoe was found in a class room cupboard after which the school returned to a degree of normality.

Though several suspects were hauled to Grimbo office the identity of the prankster was never revealed.

Back to the staff

The head teacher Mr Patrick Hagan lived on the Ford estate in Appleby Drive and was never the object of any pranks and was a really respected man.

Mr Dolan who took Spanish was a regular visitor to the Ford estate in his sports car visiting his girlfriend's house and he would always wave and acknowledge us.

My last form teacher in 4T Mr McShane who we nicknamed Sammy for whatever reason was an ever present on the estate as his family lived at the junction of Randall Drive and Simons Croft.

His brother Stephen was of the same age as and associated with us.

I liked Mr McShane he was a fair teacher and showed a genuine interest in your wellbeing.

Mr Collins helped me through my early secondary years as he had picked up on my distress in school due to issues at home.

'Sir my mum and dad are getting divorced, my dad said I'm now the man of the house but I'm only twelve' He once asked my parents to attend the school but they never came and he encouraged me to do the things that I enjoyed and coached me through the athletics.

I went back to St Thomas Aquinas to see Mr McShane and Mr Collins when I had a day off as an apprentice and they received me warmly. I had never forgotten the positives those two teachers had instilled in me.

As Mayor of Sefton I visited St Ambrose Barlow which was now the RC secondary school as the former St Thomas Aquinas boys only school and St Catherine's girls' schools had closed and Mr Dolan was teaching at the school.

We discussed my time at St Thomas Aquinas and he would refer to me as Mr Mayor and me to him as Sir at which he would say 'Mr Mayor please address by my first name'

I never could and similarly when I would meet former Royal Marine officers that I had served under with the same response 'Bob call me' and their first name offered

But I never could.

Penmaenmawr

The four years that I was at St Thomas Aquinas passed quickly but was full of lots of hilarity one such occasion was the weekend away at a camp site near Conway. I had taken ill in school and was sat on a chair in reception when one of the art teachers Mr Rathbone came down to see how I was and to tell me the good news that I was one of the six boys that were chosen to go to the weekend camp all of the class having to write a short essay on why we would like to go the weekend camp.

I was delighted and so we left on the Friday night six of us and three teachers Messrs. Rathbone, Brown and Murphy, we were given a list of clothing that included jeans and boots.

The order of the day was Dr Marten air wear boots and Wrangler or Lee jeans. I of course was treated to the poorer monkey boots and a pair of jeans called Cayuse that had a cowboy and lasso on a horse.

The Cayuse were a North American people that lived in Washington state and Oregon and it was also a name given to a wild horse taken to the New world by the Spanish in the 16th century and like me the horse was small and stocky though the history of the native Americans did not spare my then embarrassment.

I was talking about St Thomas Aquinas to our airport transfer driver James a couple of years ago and he was in the same class and also one of the six boys though we never recognised each other we recalled the trip and were able to update each other on what happened to many of our class mates.

On the Saturday of the trip we hiked up to the summit of Mount Snowdon then on the Sunday we trekked across the hills to Conway castle.

Regrettably for the teachers our visit coincided with a party of public-school boys some of whom on hearing our accents decided to pour scorn on us.

That resulted in our hurling hands full of gravel at them following which they beat a hasty retreat cursing us as ruffians as we cheered their leaving, further lobbing gravel at them from the castle ramparts.

'But sir we were defending the school'

That was not the only encounter with public school boys as one winter the school heating boiler broke and we were all sent home for the day.

Several of us set off for Ince woods were on the boundary walls there was white crosses painted at intervals were funeral processions would stop to rest and those crosses are still visible today.

There was once stood a tall wooden cross somewhere between Ince Blundell and Lunt that my friends decided to hoist me up onto with me being the smallest.

As I was being hoisted up we heard a shout 'You boys what do you think you are doing'

Turning there was a man who looked very much like Foggy from Last of the summer wine dressed very similar and carrying a walking cane.

'Get down off there at once'

'What are you doing around here you should be in school, I bet you are all playing truant aren't you?'

'The boiler is broke and we have been given the day off school' says I

'Boiler broke that's a likely story and what school is this?'

'The Tommie's' replied I followed in unison with 'St Thomas Aquinas'

'Never heard of it be off with you'

'Aye mister you can't tell us where we can and can't go' said Ronnie

'Well we shall see I will call the police'

'Fuck off' said Ged

'Disgraceful, you bunch of good for nothing Liverpool louts'
'Were from Bootle' we replied
'That's bloody worse' was his reply
We broke into rapturous laughter
'I shall have the police after you' and so, we all mooned him
'Shameful behaviour' 'shameful' as he walked briskly on
We returned the comment with a slapping of our backsides like a scene in the film Braveheart as he turned to look back at us, waving his came wildly in the air.
We took off across farmland and came out somewhere in Virgins lane, Thornton.
A few public-school boys were passing us and we asked them the time, none of us possessing a watch.
'Hey what time is?' asked Ronnie
'It is 15.45 sir' came the reply at which point we all burst out laughing at being addressed as sir which left them looking bewildered.
'What does he mean 15.45?' said Ged
'it's quarter to four thicko' replied Barry
'Why the fuck didn't he say that then' replied Ged as he lunged a punch at Barry.
The public-school boys, momentarily forgotten were then subject to expletives and the odd stone before we commenced the long walk home, Ged and Barry having ended their daily punch up.
We stopped off at a shop on the crescent in Thornton and clubbed together to buy a bottle of lemonade which we swapped around and some loose cigarettes for the few smokers inclusive of Ged and Barry.
Of course, our presence was soon reported and a number of youths came charging around the corner but fled when Ged decided to run at them.
I read some war books by Sven Hassle about his time in the German army during the second world war and I can relate to those characters and my close friends, Ged of course would be Obergefreiter Wolfgang Creutzfeldt (Tiny) the enormous Hamburger. Ged had no front teeth and would not go the dentist and he looked fearsome.

We arrived home unscathed having to also navigate the Pendle Drive estate which was also bandit country but my friends were afraid of nothing and I think the challenge excited them.

I loved going to Ince Blundell and always wanted to venture inside the grounds of the hall where there was a small heronry but for some reason we never ventured over the walls as there was always some activity going on and people out walking .

Many years later my good friend and neighbour Ralph James who was the first Labour councillor for Manor ward took me on a tour of the ward including inside Ince Blundell hall and the surrounding woods something I had always wanted to see as a child

Back to the teaching staff

The other teachers I remember are Mr Myers who picked the original school football team that included me.

Mr Bibby who took geography and was an Everton fan and you could discuss the derby matches with him.

Mr Wolfarth who took English and played the organ in the Holy Ghost church and would give you four lashes of the cane for interrupting his class.

Mr Shepherd who took science and took no nonsense in class and would grab you by your sideburns if growing any and say 'you are a horrible little man, what are you?'

'A horrible little man sir'

Afterwards you would be caned

Mr Cullen whom I think taught metal work

Mr Jackman taught carpentry but also had the misfortune of managing class 3/4D

We had to back every single book with wallpaper and one boy came in having backed his in cowboys and Indians

'It was the only role of paper in the loft sir'

'Get it off and see if someone can give you some paper'

I fail to see why books needed to be backed as in a few hours they were covered in Liverpool FC or Everton FC etc.

Worst was to leave your books in a classroom as they would be targeted and found with lewd drawings all over them and occasionally the teachers name and further lewd comments.

'Sir someone has drawn on my books and you get a mention'

Return to Penmaenmawr

During the school summer holidays, I encouraged my friends to go camping to Wales and eight of us went for a week. We had no tent but the Jehovah witness family in Hampshire avenue loaned us their bell tent for a 50p donation.

We arrived on the Saturday afternoon having been brought in two cars reluctantly by my dad and a neighbour.

We paid for a week's pitch and were read the riot act. The first night was windy with heavy rain and we spent most of that night fetching boulders from a stream to keep the tent sides down.

We met up with two boys from Ellesmere port who had come with their parents so we now totaled ten in number.

On the Monday a bus arrived with a number of girls from a convent school near Manchester accompanied by several nuns and a couple of priests.

The girls on hearing our Liverpool accents would try and mimic us and we spent the day chasing each other around and they would sneak into our tent late at night and stay for hours.

On the Wednesday me and two others were sat outside the tent the rest having gone the shower block.

One of the nuns came bounding over wielding a leather strap cursing us and making it clear what she would do with the strap if we went near the girls again only to be met by a tirade of abuse from my two friends not of the catholic faith.

The nun turned and stormed off, shortly afterwards the priests came over and said 'anymore out of you lot and we will beat you to within an inch of your life'

Before they could say anymore the rest of our mates and the two boys from Ellesmere Port returned at which point the priests scarpered followed by the usual abuse.

Later that day the girls party left the campsite and we were given our marching orders which meant my dad and the other parent coming to Wales to collect us which did not go down well and I was grounded for the remainder of the summer holidays.

I should add that we had been warned by the camp site owner for playing the radio too loud.

The T-Rex song 'Get it on' was the radio Luxembourg power play record that was played every hour on the hour and it would boom from our tent at unsociable hours.

The average day in St Tommie's

It all started with assembly the usual prayers, couple of notices then the marching up of the mornings unfortunates onto the stage to be publicly flogged in front of the school each in turn to be told how they had let the school down. I was speaking to a former Bootle Grammar school pupil and when telling him of the daily caning and how those at the receiving end had let the school down, he nearly choked on his sandwich and when composed uttered the words

'How the hell could anyone let that school down, no offence Bobby but the best thing that happened to it was when it got burnt to the ground'

The Tommie's is mentioned on the Bootle Times forum with one former Warwick Bolam pupil commenting that the mere mention of that school makes the hairs on his neck stand on edge. Another mentioned having to regularly run the gauntlet of the Tommie's. And yet to those of us that went to the school it was four years of fun and many of us went onto forge professional careers.

After assembly and the caning ritual, we would file out to our classes, 4T being at the top of the building and you would have to watch were you walked as those that had got up the stairs before you would spit down the stairwell.

The less informed would be caught standing in the line of fire including new members of the teaching staff.

The kicking of a class room door was an everyday event with the teachers always running down a stair while the perpetrator had run up a stair. It never happened on the top floor as it was usually our class that was responsible. However, our class never broke the fire alarm glass which went off occasionally to the annoyance of teachers and pupils alike if it was a cold day. Having to muster in the play grounds shivering till the fire service had given the all clear. Needless to say, the offender was nine times out of ten from class 3/4D and had been sent to get chalk or something.

One day we were in class and it was nearly 2PM when suddenly one of the class 3/4 D pupils emerged from the long jump sand pit on the far side of the school field having fell asleep in it at lunch time. 'Good god I doubt anyone knew he is missing' said the teacher before turning back to the board and writing more questions

Secondary school meals

The meals in secondary school were slightly better than in primary school and you did get chips on a Friday so worth staying for.

The first day I went into the dining hall after starting at the school I was walking with my plate to a table when suddenly I was upended and the plate went crashing to the floor and I was laying there while all around there was raucous laughter.

I had been tripped up and wanted the world to end. From that day forward, I would walk down the centre of the dining hall evading any would be trippers.

My attending school meals was somewhat ad-hoc and I never stayed at all after my youngest sister Joan started primary school.

I would have to collect her each lunch time and then get the spare house key from a neighbour.

We would have four rounds of white bread and a small jar of Shippams salmon spread paste to put on them.

Sometimes I would take a couple more slices only to be accused later as my mother would count the slices and you were not allowed the crust being reserved for my father.

Sometimes if he never came home the by now stale crust went in the bin even the starlings and house sparrows never got a look in.

Occasionally I would go straight to my friends' houses after school with a guaranteed feast, well chips and egg with brown sauce and as much bread as you wanted.

My mother sometimes sent me to the co-op butchers to ask for any Scragg ends for the dog but they were tossed in a pan with a concoction of carrots and potatoes and passed off as a stew though I much preferred half a tin of Cross and Blackwell scotch broth.

Once I was in my friend's house and his mother brought in a whole coffee cream cake from Sayers and I was the only want that liked it.

The following day Tony my friend brought in the cake which had only three slices missing two of which were what I had eaten and I put it in my desk and gorged on it all day through lessons.

I once asked my mum could she get a coffee cream cake to be looked at puzzlingly as if to say and when have you ever had such a cake.

School prefect

I mentioned earlier about my days as a milk monitor in primary school and me and Paul in our final year at the Tommie's were appointed school prefects and tasked with reporting late arrivals for assembly with those unfortunate to arrive after the school bell sounded doomed to stand outside Mr Griffiths office, no excuses just whack now back to your class.

Of course, putting us as prefects on the doors was akin to putting a rat in charge of the cheese larder and we thus had a lucrative extortion racket going.

'Let us in please'

'No, you're going to Mr Griffiths office' or Grimbo as he was known to all

And so, we traded lateness for tuck shop monies.

However once bitten twice shy and we would seldom see the same victim again other than one boy which resulted in our downfall and public flogging.

That boy who really should not have been going the tuck shop and nicknamed slim for obvious reasons was regularly caught after the bell having had to take his sister to school first.

Slim would reluctantly hand over his tuck shop monies and this continued for about two weeks. Then one morning he was marched into the school yard by his mother who started wagging her finger at us as she walked past the side door heading to the main entrance.

We were sat in class when a knock came on the door and a younger age pupil came in and said 'sir Mr Griffiths want to see' naming me and Paul.

'What have you two been up to' said our teacher 'Dunno sir' but we both knew we had been rumbled and of course it was bullying so we deserved all that was coming.

On arriving at Grimbo's office there stood a worried looking slim and his morbidly obese mother.

After Grimbo gave the customary apologies to slim and his mother for having to come to the school we were told to stand against the wall and put our hands out. We both received four whacks of the cane two on each hand.

Slim winced at every lash but his mother clearly enjoying the spectacle was salivating from the mouth.

The following morning, we were summoned on to the stage after assembly stripped of our prefect badges like a scene from the western series 'Branded' were Chuck Connors was stripped of his cavalry rank and his sword broken in two.

Then another two lashings each of the cane meaning we had been administered six of the best thankfully not all at once as our fingers were still smarting from the previous day's punishment.

Our form teacher who along with the other teachers watched the daily ceremony with disinterest simply said to us afterwards 'Guess you boys will not want to be going near the deputy's office in a hurry'

'No sir' we replied, we had however become somewhat folk heroes in the school once the story got around about the extortion racket.

We would regularly be placed on detention, if caught staring out the window at a class football match or when a local girl's school would use the field for their sports day.

You were given a democratic choice, the cane or detention and I had little choice than to request the cane as I had a paper round to deliver.

Only once did a teacher refuse to cane me saying he reserved such punishment for more befitting crimes and gave me detention.

I must not stare out the window during class, which had to be written 100 times neatly.

'Done it sir, can I go now'

'Brennan sit down it is only 4.20 you still have ten minutes left'

Ironically, I would use the remaining time staring out the window at Grimbo whacking a golf ball.

Social life after school

Starting secondary school opened the door to friendships with boys from other areas with eleven plus failures arriving at St Tomas Aquinas from Holy Ghost, Our Lady of Walsingham, St Benet's, Holy Rosary all Netherton and Old Roan schools but also some came from St James in Bootle.

From these new friendships you would   venture to the localities of the feeder schools and start to see girls and the rest they say is history.

Unfortunately, the period of secondary school was also a period of violence not just at football matches but between different areas where you would be attacked if found in another gangs area very much like the American cult film 'the Warriors' trying to get to their own turf unscathed.

There would be regular violent battles between adolescents from Netherton against Litherland and Seaforth.

Ford as an estate was caught smack in the middle of the warring factions and many a night you would have to flee across the golf course to escape the gangs that would rampage through the estate.

One notorious gang the 'Freelance' consisted of mainly teenagers but also several well-known head cases in their early twenties that clearly enjoyed dishing out violence.

The late sixties early seventies were dominated by Skinheads, Mods that I later became and Greasers including a Hells Angels chapter called the Crosby 1 per cent along with peaceful folk loving music types such as Troggs and Hippies a real melting pot of social cultures.

Some of the local hippies set off in a battered van to set up their own commune but returned a week later the attempt an abject failure as they had no land in which to set up the commune or monies to sustain themselves.

One of the hippies reminded me of Neil from 'the young ones' and told us

'We are going to live off the land man'

He used to come and chat with us in his army greatcoat, floral neck scarf and Loons pants looking out of sorts as we all wore parallel trousers, Flemings jeans, parkas and Crombie's and the occasional trilbi hat.

Some lads from the Park lane estate or Dodge as it was known thought it rather strange and not in keeping with our chosen culture asked

'Why the fuck does he hang around with you'? followed by 'fucking weirdo'

We had no answer to that other than we never minded him, besides it was the greasers and the Crosby 1 per cent we loathed.

Eventually the character Neil likely having had his fill of insults ceased to associate with us.

I would later see him in Technical college but we never spoke it was as if we were strangers.

I loved everything about Mod culture, with Trojan Reggae music along with Tamla Motown, Atlantic and Northern soul but I also liked folk music with the likes of Bob Dylan, and Judy Collins and of course David Bowie.

The Bowie albums Aladdin Sane and Hunky Dory both masterpieces that me Ged and Barry would sit and listen too for hours in Geds house in between re-enacting scripts from Monty Pythons flying Circus 'I'm a lumber jack and I'm okay' and we would finish off any conversation with 'and now for something completely different'

We would wear Como brogue shoes or plain Comos which my mother took me to the co-op store in Netherton to buy a pair. It did not matter that they were Comos you still had to say you got them from another shoe shop. There was a cobbler lived in Musker Drive and he would fit steel tips to the heel of each shoe for a small amount.

Everyone started wearing Jaytex button down shirts from Eric's but my mother bought me in a lime green bri-nylon button down shirt from TJ Hughes that caused me immense shame when forced to wear it.

Birds eggs was still a pastime of many boys into the first two years of secondary school and once four of us were cutting through Ford cemetery on our way to the fun fair that was held each year on Moss lane school field when Ronnie spotted a woodpecker going into a hole in a tall tree.

As the gangs designated tree climber, I declined on this occasion as I wanted to get to the fair.

Ged unimpressed with my refusal handed Ronnie his Observer book of Birds eggs and proceeded slowly up the tree trying in vain to get his hand into the hole which the spotted woodpecker had now flown out of. Ged proceeded to slowly climb down and was cursing me for putting him in that predicament.

'This is your fucking fault Bobby'

As Ged was clearly struggling, Ronnie issued directions 'The branch is just below you Ged'

Before me and Barry could shout 'stop as there was no branch just below, Ged lost his balance and landed on a grave stone

'Fucking hell Geds dead' said Ronnie

'Well he is in the right placed laughed Barry'

Ged of course was out cold, his cheek was embedded in Green stones

I stood there wondering what to do next when Ronnie said 'I'm off to the fair'

'We can't just leave him here' said I when a couple came rushing over at which Barry said 'he will be okay now let's go'

'Excuse me' said the woman 'you can't just walk off and leave him' I shrugged my shoulders and gave her Geds name and address and followed Ronnie and Barry who were now hurling abuse at the church warden who always chased us when using the cemetery as a short cut home. Later that afternoon I called to Geds house to see how he was and to return his Birds eggs book, his brother informed me that Ged in hospital but okay.

A few days later Ged came home and immediately set about seeking revenge. I was spared a thrashing as I had returned the prized birds egg book which took some persuasion as Ronnie insisted on keeping it saying Ged would think it was lost. Well leaving Ged on the grave was one thing keeping his book was another and I was not having any part of it.

The Observer book of bird's eggs was a very informative book but we would often on finding a nest look at what egg it resembled and say it was one of those.

We seldom seen the bird vacate the nest so relied heavily on the book, and of course we had eggs that we claimed were that of a Chough or Siskin which were not possible.

I think our greatest claim as egg collectors was to possess eggs that we believed were a cross between a blackbird and a song thrush and we claimed to have evidence of cross breeding that took place solely on a derelict farm in Lydiate. One morning we decided to revisit the farm but stopped at the rookery in Brickwall lane Sefton which was of course the old rectory and now the site of a small exclusive housing development at Glebe End.

Climbing over the wall I was ordered up the tree to a rook's nest and having placed one egg in my mouth descended and repeated the action about four times.

We then walked through the rookery to a stream at the rear of the site that led to St Helens well and we found about half a dozen geese eggs that were cold and had clearly been deserted. Breaking one the smell was appalling very much like the stink bombs let off in school. We opted to take the rest and worry about how to blow them when we got home. I had a Liverpool bag and they were placed in the bag and we carried on to Lydiate.

On arriving at the farm, we set about searching the shrubs that surrounded the derelict green houses and ventured onto the edge of a cabbage field to get past some obstacle but were unknowingly spotted by the farmer.

As so often when you are out for the day the need to have a crap would happen and the only means of cleaning oneself was to use dock leaves or whatever was around. Dock leaves were also good for the nettle stings that we always suffered, well psychologically they helped.

On this occasion me and Barry both needed a crap so we found some old paint cans and both set about the process of emptying our bowels having acquired dock leaves and some old netting off the greenhouses.

Unfortunately, we were not afforded the luxury of having a crap in peace as the others decided to throw stones at the paint cans we were sat on and you just had to endure it till they decided to leave you in peace.

Then we heard a shout 'what the bloody hell are you doing on here, you are trespassing' It was the farmer who was about six-foot-tall and broad as hell and wielding a cane.

Just as the others were explaining that we were looking for birds eggs me and Barry appeared from behind a greenhouse me carrying my bag.

'What have you got in that bag'? 'open it now' which I did revealing the bird's eggs. I was then ordered to take the eggs out and place them on the floor.

'Where are you lot from'

'Ford in Bootle' I replied'

'You don't get eggs like this in Bootle' said the farmer

'we got them from Sevo 'said Ged, Sevo meaning Sefton

'Well clear off now' said the farmer and' it's a good job you never had any of my cabbages in that bag'

'What the fuck do we want with cabbages' said Ronnie
'I don't like cabbage' said me,
'Get the hell off here now you cheeky little bastards' followed by
'You are bloody lucky I don't give you this' waving his cane
In a flash Ged picked up one of the eggs and threw it, hitting the side of farmers head the smell was horrendous and we legged it off the site leaving my Liverpool bag behind.

Running up the road we hid on Robbins island on the Northway for about half an hour then assuming the coast was clear set off for home.

The trek home involved the usual cursing of anyone that passed us and Ged and Barry fighting over who had the last drag of the ciggy.

I had the ordeal of explaining the lost Liverpool bag and was thus grounded for a week. Being grounded was akin to house arrest and I was not even allowed to speak to my friends at the door.

How I wanted to just be lashed and then let out it, it seemed the punishment was unique to me as my friends would often comment on how bad my parents were.

The strict regime did though keep me out of trouble as my friends were arrested during the week for commandeering a tractor from a field in Thornton driving it up Lydiate lane to be arrested at the Cabbage Inn but looking back I believe the punishment meted out to me was excessive.

One night we were cutting through the cemetery and heading for the wall that we would scale dropping down onto Sterrix lane when Stephen another friend said 'Hey there's someone in them bushes over there'

Creeping over we found a discarded pair of trousers that Stephen reached in and there was a wallet and car keys.

On hearing no further sound from the bushes, we climbed onto the wall at Sterrix lane and sat astride the top of the wall for about ten minutes. Still hearing no sound, we climbed down and Stephen shared out the contents being about £25 pounds and then dropped the car keys into a grid.

There was no address or photographs in the wallet and he was never taking it to the police station and so it remained a mystery as to who they belonged to and how on earth the they managed to get home.

The Convent orchard

The convent of the Good Shepherd in Sterrix Lane closed in the early seventies and was knocked down but the orchard remained for a couple of years and we would raid the orchard which had countless apple trees and a large pear tree.

The church warden would make vain attempts to capture us but there would be in the region of about fifty boys and girls raiding that orchard and we never did any damage in the cemetery it was unheard of then.

One early evening we were waiting to carry out another raid when Group Four security turned up as they were looking after what was left off the site and they would leave a German shepherd dog in a kennel at the site.

Whatever use it was locked up it was hardly a deterrent and Ged decided to investigate how menacing the dog was which barked furiously as he approached the kennel.

We started to climb into the orchard when Ged clambered on top of the kennel and undid the bolt which sent the dog hurtling in our direction.

It stood barking and snarling up at us as we sat safe on the wall when someone decided to shout Ged. The dog stopped snarling at us its ears stood up and it turned and spotted Ged and made off towards him. The nearest tree was about five yards from Ged so he made a dash for it and climbed up it with the dog now snarling at him from the base of the tree.

Despite several attempts to lure the dog away from Ged it would run a few yards then turn back and stand guard under the tree again.

Ged remained in the tree till group four returned about an hour later and was brought down from the tree but once the dog was locked in the back of the van he ran and made for the wall. The driver of the van too old to give chase pursued Ged around Poulsom Drive in the van stopping to question us as we sat on a wall in Carr Meadow Hey, rolling down the window 'bet it was you lot on the convent site' followed by 'If I see you on there again I will let the dog after you'

'Fuck off'

Which he did and we continued to raid the orchard intermittently over the next few weeks till we got bored.

Most of the orchard raiders were school friends that lived off the estate. One friend Mark arrived having walked from Netherton in a pair of football boots as his shoes were only for school.

I met Mark again years later when he was working in Hartwood Hosiery in Skelmersdale.

My mother was a kitchen assistant and Mark introduced himself to her and I arranged to see him one lunch time and the orchard and football boots came up in the conversation.

When back in school we were paid a visit by priests from the Catholic seminary at Montford college in Up-Holland with stories of the facilities and grounds. All in all, it was to recruit to the priesthood but the grounds seemed ideal for birds egging so I went home and asked

'Can I go to Montford college'

My mother asked 'is this like Salesian college that you should have gone to instead of where you are now? 'never forgetting the shame brought upon her for my failed eleven plus.

'No, it is a priest's college I replied

Now given their determination that I attend confession and Sunday mass I was surprised by their response.

'You are not going to be a priest' said my mother

'Forget it soft lad' said my father

I did not go and so there would be no Bishop Brennan outside of Craggy island.

As we got older the interest in birds' eggs was replaced by the interest in girls and having made friends from other areas we would go to parties but there was never any damage because you had respect for any home that you were invited. There remained the violence that afflicted neighbourhoods and football terraces and if you met a girl from Litherland you would be putting yourself at risk of walking to her home. Similarly, with our paper rounds we would have to go to Dillon's in Thornton each Sunday afternoon to take our collections and be paid. We all had order bikes and would double up for the journey with one riding the bike the other sat in the carrier at the front and it was at least safety in numbers.

There were a couple of girls working in the shop and though we never spoke with them at the time one of them would one day become my wife.

During the summer holidays we would spend a lot of time playing football on the Greenie or frequenting the piggeries where we would bake potatoes taken from the farmers field.

Our fires were always lit in an elevated position so we could see anyone approaching from Whites farm.

Ged came up with the idea that we were sent to protect the song thrush population and proclaimed that we were now the song thrush brigade.

You greeted Geds daft ideas with laughter but compliance. Ged made me number one with him being my 2IC and a new recruit Franny number three.

Barry not being allowed into the brigade became leader of the Black bird brigade the arch enemy along with his number two another lad whose mother was German having met his father when he was in the British army on the Rhine and he would be subject to the usual Adolf jokes.

We even had our own oath of allegiance 'I promise to obey the honour of the song thrush against all others' the downside was the induction ceremony where you had to sport an old birds' nest on your head for the duration of the time in the piggeries.

This usually meant a couple of hours having to sit around the fire roasting potatoes wearing the new regulation head gear.

On days when it was too hot to play football we would jump in the canal but had to take a bag of salt for the leeches that often found you.

We would also go to Melwood and sit on an electricity generator building to watch Liverpool train and obtain autographs as the players arrived and they were always along with Bill Shankly receptive to our requests for their autographs.

Looking back at those times It is not just being nostalgic because anyone of my generation will attest to the summers being endless hot days of warmth. The seasons were predictable not like today with the effects of climate change.

When the canal was frozen over we would slide on the ice and dare each other to walk over the thin ice but none of us were that foolish.

I learnt not to go on the ice while Ged and Barry remained on the bank because they would hurl heavy rocks and once a beer keg onto the ice.

The beer keg came from the back of the old Holy Ghost parochial club that we would regularly go behind taking turns to drink from one of the kegs.

One scam that we had going was the lemonade bottle returns and the chip shop in Carr Meadow Hey was the mark. We would take turns in returning a bottle which would be brought to the back of the shop were one of us would retrieve it and bring back around to the front, the back door always open.

It was working quite well till one of our gang Jimmy decided to write Jimi LFC on the label and it was picked up on the third circuit and that was the end of the scam.

You could get a small bag of left-over chips from the chippie all the crispy ones from the bottom of the fryer and it would only cost sixpence. We always shared the chips and no one was ever left out if it meant you only had a few chips each, we even shared bubble gum.

My final days at St Thomas Aquinas were one of mixed emotions as I was going to Bootle Technical college in September having passed the entrance examination.

On the Thursday we had the Bootle schools' athletics at Stuart road sports fields and I was representing the school in the 1500 metres followed shortly after by the 400 x 100 metre relay and I was the first leg runner.

I finished second in the 1500 metre relay to a boy from St Joan's who later became a fellow student in college.

Mr Collins our athletics teacher was overseeing the race and said to me 'I will say on your marks get set then blow my whistle, but when you hear get set start running' I stood there with the baton in my hand, on your marks get set, but I stood still and waited for the whistle that came a second later.

I was very fast at running and I just concentrated on my leg of the race.

I could feel the wind passing by my face as I ran handing over the baton I looked back and the lead that had been opened up was a sight to behold I felt overwhelmed.

Unfortunately, our third leg faltered and was soon caught but we did finish second and our athletics team had accumulated enough points to retain the Bootle school's athletics trophy.

The following day being the last day of school we were called up on stage to receive our certificates and each boy was applauded then they left the stage.

Mr Collins held me back as I had two certificates to receive and he said to the assembly. 'Robert leaves the school today he ran two brilliant races yesterday and we are all very proud of him and wish him well for the future'.

That afternoon we had the final days film showing 'Murphy's war' with Peter O'Toole which was interrupted midway through by Ged and Barry having yet another fight and so I said goodbye to St Thomas Aquinas school.

I was often late returning to school after lunch because of Ged and Barry as they would seek to prove who was the hardest on the day and I of course had to referee the fight, my decision often leading to a return fight.

Lewis clothing factory

Before I received the result of the entrance exam to Bootle Technical college and with the uncertainty of passing, me and Paul went to the Lewis clothing factory in Beach road, Litherland to train as machinists, having seen the advert in the Echo.

On arriving a woman came out and took one look at us saying sarcastically

'Why do you two want to be machinists'

'We need a job' said Paul

'Well only young ladies work on the machines and you two do not look like young ladies to me' came the reply

'It never mentioned young ladies in the Echo' said Paul

She took our details and walked off

'I was just about to tell her to fuck off' said Paul

A few weeks later and still no result of the entrance exam to Bootle Technical college I asked Paul if he had heard.

As he had not heard he rang up Lewis to be told that if we had not heard from them after two weeks of the interview we had not been successful.

'Well that's it then Paul' said me

I never seen Paul again till we were renting a house in Galsworthy Avenue around about 1990 when Sefton council were doing external works to the rented houses.

Paul was employed by Sefton direct works and was working on our home and we reminisced about our youths.

No longer afterwards Paul was made redundant when Sefton council scrapped the direct works as a budget saving.

For information Lewis was opened in 1856 at number 44 Ranelagh Street in 1856 exactly 100 years before I was born by David Lewis who was born David Levy.

When I started technical college most of my friends had gone to Scotts bakery in Netherton as van lads and had money to spend but my mother forbade me from going even temporarily and would say

'you will have a trade not like them'

I gave up my paper round on starting in Bootle Technical College and enrolled on a pre-apprentice building course which was one year in duration.

The course included Technical drawing, Painting & Decorating, Carpentry & Joinery, Plumbing and Bricklaying. On a Friday we would have morning lectures then go to Balliol baths or Bootle South boys club for five a side in the afternoon. I enjoyed Technical college and befriended many lads including some from Litherland and the infamous 'Freelance' and I was then able to cross into the hitherto no-go area of Litherland and the Pendle drive estate unscathed.

One of my college friends Les had a brother who was the Sergeant-in-arms for the Crosby 1 per cent now fancy that. Another college friend Peter became a left-handed bricklayer and had played drums in the band 'The Melody makers' the group that the late Liverpool comedian Tom O'Connor formed from pupils at St Joan's school.

I considered bricklaying and had an opportunity of gaining an apprenticeship with Costain's but developed a greater interest in painting & decorating and there was so much to learn, lincrusta and flock wall papers and sign writing that I mastered learning of all the different brushes named after birds. Such was my enthusiasm I attended night school at the college and Southport art school.

I returned to helping out with early morning milk deliveries which enabled me to go to see Liverpool as it was only about 50p to get into the kop at the time. The kop was full of about 25,000 locals from Liverpool and you could not move and had to take a pee where you stood. I loved standing on the kop terraces and would look at the younger fans in the boys pen and feel their despair having spent two years in that corner of the ground with its 'give us your programme and we will make sure no one harms you' and the frequent fights.

We bought a massive union jack flag from the Army & Navy stores in Church Street and ironed on the words Liverpool and kop rules for the last day of the 1972/73 season when we won the first division.

The flag has featured on some photos of the kop overtime but I do not know what became of it as none of us brought it home after the match as we all at some point during the match had to go to the St John Ambulance office as we had all been drinking in the Park hotel disco on the Friday night. Once you had left the middle of the kop you had no chance of getting back there again.

We would all congregate in the middle of the kop and start the singing which continued from before kickoff till the final whistle and you would be hoarse by the end of the game.

We would obtain derby match tickets from the father of Everton reserve goalkeeper Andy Rankin who lived in Hampshire Avenue. You would be in the Anfield road end with the Everton fans or the Gwladys Street it never mattered you could wear your red scarf and no one bothered you there was not the bitterness that some fans have today.

I often wondered why things changed and have never really got a definitive answer but some have said it was due to English clubs being expelled from Europe after the Heysel tragedy and I think the Everton team of the day would have won the European cup.

Notwithstanding rivalry both clubs' supporters came together as one after Hillsborough.

I had owned two scarves one from the 1970s which I tied in the link of scarves from Anfield across Stanley park to Goodison after the tragedy but my very first 1960s scarf I tied to a crash barrier on the kop and wept and swore to never stand on the terraces again.

We do as a city come together when faced with attacks from the establishment and who can ever forget the collusion, lies and smears that followed the Hillsborough tragedy. It took decades for the truth to come out but apologies mean nothing there can never be justice without the criminal prosecutions of those responsible.

Even before the Hillsborough tragedy Thatcher despised the city with some of her ministers holding the opinion that Liverpool should be left to a 'managed decline' though, give Michael Heseltine his due he at least tried and genuinely cared about Liverpool despite Thatcher telling him he was wasting his time.

Finally, on Thatcher why will no government hold an enquiry or order an independent review into the miner's strike and the events that occurred in June 1984 at the Orgreave coking plant in South Yorkshire?

My sister Mary moved out of the family home in Ford and went to live with my Grandad and June in Skelmersdale and met and married Peter the son of my grandad and Junes neighbours Charlie and Marge. Charlie being a leading member of the trade's council and UCATT union in Skelmersdale.

He was a man who worked tirelessly to better the lives of those in Skelmersdale. Charlie and Marge originated from Middlesbrough and were lifelong communists.

During the second world war in Italy Charlie being a red was sent out on reconnaissance missions not expected to return.

My brother in law Peter was a coal miner and one of just a few from his Nottingham pit that went on strike.

After the strike was over his name and those of the others were inscribed on the NUM branch banner which the Union of Democratic Mineworkers confiscated.

He eventually left the pit which closed along with 120 others over the following years. Irrespective of what people thought of Arthur Scargill he was right when he warned all the pits would close. My wife Lesley and I had the honour of marching alongside Arthur and his wife on the pit closure marches in the early 1990s when Bold and Sutton Manor faced closure.

Back to the home

My father would come home every other Tuesday night and some Saturday day times. Each Saturday I would meet up with my friends at the shops in Carr Meadow Hey and we would all jump the 56 bus up to the Mons or sometimes the 52 bus to Spellow lane and walk the rest of the way to the ground up sleeper's hill to the kop.

One Saturday my father came in and ordered me to watch my sister Joan as he was going on a message.

'I'm supposed to meet my mates to go the match dad'

'You do as your told and mind Joan till I come back, okay'

He then went out the door and took a short cut through the flats to my mother's friend or rather his friend.

As it was nearly 12.30 I told my sister that I was just going to tell my mates I would see them at the ground and I would be straight back.

I just arrived at the shops where we always met up less than five minutes from home when someone said

'Bobby there's your dad' turning around I was shocked to see him sitting in his car and gesturing for me to get in.

I was nearly 16 my father was 37 and as I got in the car he said

'What did I fucking tell you about staying in'

Before I could respond he lashed out at my face with his left hand and his signet ring caught me on the lip. Blood started flowing down my chin and onto my shirt and looking up with tears in my eyes I could see the shocked looks on my friends faces.

On pulling up at the square there was a few neighbours talking at the gates and a lot of children playing out. My father just walked past not acknowledging anyone pushing

me forward as I held my hand over my mouth, the neighbours falling quiet as we walked to the house.

I was sent to my room and when my mother came home from work my father left almost immediately as he was a compare at Courtaulds club where he was now working in Aintree.

My mother came into my room and took one look at me and said

'Have you been fighting again?'

'No mum my dad hit me'

'Well you must have deserved it then'

I asked if I could go out but was told 'you will have to ask your father'

'How can I ask him, he won't probably be here now till next week' and so I was grounded till college on Monday.

My father had taken a second job as a private hire taxi driver and a few days later his driver window had been shattered and he ordered me out the house saying 'your mates, that gang you hang around with will know whose done this' then added 'they probably tried to rob the taxi radio and got disturbed '

I informed my friends that someone tried to nick my dad's taxi radio and had broken his side window at which my mates started laughing and told me that they did it because of what he had done to me.

Even though what they did was wrong I smiled and said thanks and went home to tell my dad the news that they did not know who was responsible but would keep their ears open.

Though I was enjoying my time in Bootle Technical college, shortage of money aside I was in the final months of the pre-apprenticeship course and arrived home one evening to be told by my mother that I was to attend an examination to get into Chadburns on the corner of Bridle road.

We had new neighbours that moved into the former home of Jack the merchant sailor and my mother got speaking to them and was informed of the exams for electronic apprentices.

I objected and said to my mother that I do not want to go I want to be a painter & decorator but I was told

'You are bloody well going or you will answer to your father'

I pleaded with her saying that 'I will have a trade' but to no avail it was her will that I attend

'For a proper trade'

So, I had to attend but did not pass and was told, likely to spare any embarrassment that the result was borderline

That meant nothing to my mother I had once again brought shame on her.

I was interviewed for an apprenticeship with Norwest Holst housing which was based in Duinningsbridge road, were now stands a car showrooms and my mother was out telling the few neighbours who she bothered with of my successful interview.

Three-day week and blackouts

During the early 1970s the National Union of Miners called a national strike as generations of mine workers were underpaid a fact that could not be disputed. The Conservative Heath government refused to negotiate with the miners.

The strike cut supplies of coal to the power stations which produced most of the electricity. Power cuts were introduced followed by a three-day working week, the latter not just an attempt to conserve energy but to turn public opinion against the miners.

The power cuts lasted a few hours each day and were staggered so not all areas were cut off at the same time and you would look in the Liverpool Echo to read what time your area would be cut off. It would be total blackout in Ford with not even street lights lit up yet across the road in Litherland everything was bright but a few hours later it would reversed.

We would go into one of the neighbours houses during the black out as they had a gas cooker so we could have a cup of tea and every house had candles glowing. You had to make sure you had candles as they were running short in the local chandlers. There was a family in Ford whose electricity supply had been disconnected well before the power cuts. They would have candles glowing every night that resulted in some local children throwing stones at the house windows. My friends and I would chase those younger children whenever we seen it happening, even then we recognised the hardship that existed in our estate.

I was never allowed to leave the square when the power cut affected Ford but my friends would be out having a ball. Once when stood outside the neighbour's house we heard the Baines dairy electric milk float coming down the street. As one might have guessed my friends Jimmy and Ronnie were in the front seats driving it with Ged and Barry and several others sat on the back of the float.

My mother and others came out to hear the racket that included a loud singing of the Herman's Hermits song 'No milk today' I fell about laughing and received a whack of the head from my mother

'I might have known it would be your bloody friends'

Lido di Jesolo Italian Adriatic

Before starting at Norwest Holst, we went on a family holiday to Italy my mother having obtained a personal loan courtesy of her best friend.

The holiday 12 days in total 4 days of which were spent travelling to and from Italy by coach starting with the coach ride from London Victoria to Dover then the ferry across to Ostend. The sights were wonderful, Innsbruck and the Brenner pass were spectacular but I hated the stopovers and getting washed at grubby coach station and sleep was impossible of a night on the coach.

We stayed at the hotel Calypso which was owned by a guy called Mario who would proudly show you a silver Lira coin with Mussolini on it and proudly say 'El Duce' and lament how Italy was so much better then. Thinking back Mario was in his late forties and may well have supported the fascists during the war he certainly adored 'El Duce' and he appeared to get on extremely well with German tourists of around the same age as him. There was a young engaged couple from the South coast travelling with the girl's parents and they would argue all the way down to Italy. Once when I was sat with a drunk from Bolton who was telling me all sorts of bizarre tales I noticed my father making a bee line to the south coast girl to console her after she had another public argument with her fiancé who stormed out the hotel, her parents nowhere to be seen. My mother and sisters had routinely retired to bed at about 9PM each night and I watched shaking my head as my father and the young woman moved to a corner of the room. As my father gestured to the waiter for drinks he noticed me looking over and pointed up at the ceiling ordering me to get to bed. Well no way was I going up to bed so I left the hotel and went around a few bars returning a couple of hours later quite drunk to find him gone, to where I cared not a jot.

The following morning my mother and sister were down for the continental breakfast. I stayed in bed with a hangover till the maids came to change the bedding then made my way downstairs to grab a coffee.

'Where is your dad' said my mother

'Haven't see him' I replied but he would eventually surface with a newspaper

On the return coach trip the south coast couple were less argumentative the engagement seemingly back on.

Prior to going on holiday my friend's sister was selling a Tamla Motown chart hits album for £2.00 pounds and even at 16 I had to ask my mother's permission to buy it.

'Mum can I buy an LP off Tommy's sister its £2.00 pound'

'Let me see it first' she said, so I showed her the album

'Yes, I like some of those songs so you can buy it'

Going outside I said to my friend, 'my mum said I can buy it'

'Fucking hell Bobby why do you need permission'

I just shrugged my shoulders.

Tommy said his sister would not let him listen to the record and asked if he could borrow it while I was on holiday which I did.

Going back home after paying my friends sister the money my mother asked where the record was

When I told her, I had lent it to Tommy till I come back she said 'Get that back now' and so I had to fetch the record back.

Given the families financial difficulties It was puzzling that we went to Italy and the year before Spain though holidays abroad were now becoming more popular and were something to boast about.

The holidays of my childhood and the Isle of Man were to be no more.

However, they would be paying for the holidays on the never, never, adding further to their financial woes. We were shit skint but off abroad.

It was not long before my father asked me for even the little I received for helping out on milk deliveries and I felt embarrassed for him when he took just £1.25 off me.

Italy was the last of the family holidays and I don't think they ever holidayed again till my father was made redundant which was some 12 years later. My father bought a toupee that he would wear believing no one would notice but you cannot suddenly sprout a thick centre piece of hair. He continued to proudly wear his hair piece sending me around to Vernon's stores to buy double sided tape and he would dry the bloody thing with the warm air heater that was on my bedroom shelf.

I would be asleep on the odd nights he stayed and be awoken by the whirring off the heater, daring not to open my eyes.

My father would ridicule anyone that wore a wig and boast that his brother Tony would ask him why he had a full head of hair whilst Tony was completely bald.

One evening amidst a blazing row following an unknown female ringing the house my mother tugged off the toupee and threw it down the stairs.

He shouted, 'now they all know'

I tried to be helpful but my input was hardly tact in that I said 'Dad I have always known'

He picked up the toupee, cracked me to the side of the head turned and went upstairs to the bathroom to fix his crowning glory following which he left for a few days. My mother blamed me for his leaving, having forgotten all about the female caller and ordered me to my room till the following day.

My late brother in law Ronnie who was married to Lesley eldest sister Edna worked in Courtaulds and on first meeting him he was taken back when I told him my father worked there.

He of course knew my father well but he had never mentioned to Ronnie having any teenage children.

Ronnie told me that everyone knew my father wore a wig and some lads would tell him they knew.

My father had a female friend in Courtaulds, more about that later and she was likely one of many.

Before I got my scooter and if it was heavy rainfall my father would occasionally drop me off just over Sefton road bridge in Maghull by what was then Koters printers and tell me he had to pick someone up and never take me what was a mere further five minutes to Green park even in heavy rain.

When my first daughter was born he said

'I will resent her If I'm called grandad'

My mother suggested we refer to him as Bob with my sister Joan suggesting 'uncle Bob' and they would both say to my daughters 'Are you coming to see Bob' and 'uncle Bob'

I refused to allow my children to refer to him in those terms but it was lost on my mother and sister who carried on with their charade.

My mother would in later years say 'oh they always knew him as Bob'

No, they never mum!

Norwest Holst

When I started at Norwest Holst it was at Green park, Maghull but later I would be sent to Penwortham, Poulton-le-Fylde with lifts provided and having to travel from Skelmersdale to Pensby on the Wirral for 8.00AM which meant getting up at 05.30 to get a lift to Liverpool from a person that worked on the docks, and arriving home each evening at 08.30PM and this lasted for six weeks.

My first three months at Green park in Maghull was spent priming bare wood, acrylic primer for the indoor skirting boards and architraves and oil-based primary for the external wood, soffits and fascia boards.

Each day a 29-year-old labourer would come and sit and chat during the half hour lunch break or the 10-minute tea breaks that we had twice per day. I never thought anything other than he was simply being nice, but he was clearly grooming me as about 1 year later when I was waiting for a lift home with some of the labourers I was grabbed by a few of them and my trousers flung outside the site canteen hut.

I never thought anything of it as there was always pranks being played on apprentices but I was suddenly subject to a sexual assault which was witnessed by other labourers all of whom simply laughed.

After leaving Norwest I did not see the person who assaulted me again for some 20 years till as a Sefton councillor I was travelling up to Southport for a council committee meeting.

I noticed him standing at the platform of a station and felt myself sinking down into the seat so as not to be spotted. He may well have passed away now who knows and who cares certainly not me.

Notwithstanding having to keep a wary eye open for the predator who would sneak into the houses and continue with his sexual overtures as soon as Myles the foreman had left there was many funny incidents that happened on the site that made for many memorable laughs.

Norwest Holst construction owner Noel Le Mare owned the racehorse Red Rum and attended the opening of the show house on Green park, prior to which a labourer was sent in to tidy up the house.

The labourer that was sent in was an alcoholic and would hide wine bottles in the breeze blocks of houses under construction.

On the afternoon in question I was wallying (painting) walls with the regulation Magnolia emulsion when Myles the foreman called me and pointed at the show house were the Le Mare party were being comforted before being driven away.

The labourer had entered what was for him an Aladdin's cave helping himself to the bottles of Whiskey, Sherry and fine wines then some of the buffet.

Having taken his fill decided to have a nap to be awakened by the Le Mare party entering the house. He grabbed his sweeping brush ran out the show house ignoring the distraught VIPs and was later sacked.

On another occasion and shortly after a family moved in the new owner of the house came storming down to the site office having found a turd in the walk-in bedroom cupboard. Given its description of being covered in fur it had clearly been there undetected for some time. The checker who was in the site office remarked 'I bet there was no toilet paper with it'

Theft on building sites was a common problem and once the police were called by a home owner and turned up to find the security night watchman loading copper piping in to a van. As an apprentice I was witness to many such thefts once I was unloading paint deliveries and on putting two one-gallon tins of white gloss on the floor they were swooped up by one of the site agents who just put his finger over his lips and so I carried on unloading the van. Two more-gallon tins of white undercoat were swooped on by the same site agent who again put his finger over his lips.

Later that morning the checker called the foreman Myles down to the stores as there was a discrepancy in that four tins were missing. I was summoned into the site office were the site agent responsible stood arms on hips and asked me if I knew anything of the missing tins to which I shook my head.

He then said 'I suppose you would not tell us the name even if you knew who it was' and I replied 'No' and that was the end of that episode but not the thefts as 7-inch flat brushes would be traded for a fiver a go and readily disappear.

Once I was left to finish off some skirting boards after Myles went home and minutes later in came one of the civil engineers asking if I could spare some white gloss. I informed him I only had what was in my tin and he pointed at a full gallon of gloss and said 'what about that there?'

'I cannot give you any of that it's a brand-new tin and Myles will know'

He suggested that I leave the small landing window open and he will make it look like someone got in and robbed it. The following morning, I arrived on site and got the key to the house and on opening the door I was taken back as there was muddy footsteps leading up the stairs to the landing window a muddy foot print on the window ledge the small sash window still open and the gallon of white gloss had gone.

Myles came in and his first question was to ask me if I knew anything of it and I just shook my head but inside I was thinking I know who it was.

Myles went off to report the theft and once out of sight the civil engineer came over and asked 'did Myles say anything'

'He had asked me did I know anything about it and I said no' was my reply.

He then said 'nothing to worry about I made it look like someone got in the landing window and stole the paint' adding 'I took my muddy boots off when I got the top of the stairs and put them back on when I came down again and left through the door'.

I replied 'yep someone climbed up the ladder put their hand through the small sash window to open the big window. they then climbed in stole the paint and went out the same way closing the fucking big window on their way out'

He said 'that's thanks for you and here is me stopping you from getting the blame for not closing the door'.

Myles was baffled it was by all accounts a bizarre theft.

Another time I was asked by another worker to leave the small kitchen window open and the following day I came in to find every kitchen unit had gone apart from the sink unit which had its doors missing.

I would get into the van of a night time for a lift home and there would be bathroom suites covered in dust sheets.

101

Thefts of cabbages and Brussels sprouts from the farm fields was common with farmers reporting yellow dumper trucks seen on the field. However, there was about 30 yellow dumper trucks on Green park and of course everyone took the greens home.

Hobbies

I mention earlier in the book how I collected models and would hang planes from my ceiling. The very last model that I ever put together was a battle of Britain tribute featuring the spitfire and hurricane that my grandad bought me.

I was sat in my bedroom one Saturday morning painting the models when my mother shouted up the stairs 'get around the shops I need some oxo cubes' I did not reply thinking I will just finish this final wing then I will go down.

A few minutes later my mother burst into my room with the sweeping brush   shouting

'I bloody asked you to go the shops'

I said to her that 'I was just finishing the aircraft wing' well that was that she lashed out with the sweeping brush knocking all of my model planes from the ceiling and that was the end of yet another hobby.

I had a great foreign stamp collection that included pre-war Nazi stamps and one night I was looking in a box for a football programme and realised my stamp album was not there and when I told my mother it had gone she replied

'I gave it' to naming a work colleague of hers 'as you don't bother it with anymore and her son has started collecting stamps'

Now I'm a real mod

As I was now getting paid I could afford to buy my own transport and I bought an SX150 Lambretta the crème de le crème of scooters and I would ride to work in Maghull but occasionally if it was a pleasant morning I would walk and gaze at the pheasants and partridges in the fields along Brickwall lane. Walking past the long-gone cottage of Jay Leary a local artist and taxidermist. Stopping at the rookery and thinking about my climbing the trees, was it just only 3 years ago it seemed longer. Then I thought of Perwick bay which was 7 years earlier but seemed a different life, my childhood had flown so fast I was now 17.

Me and my friends would go to the Park hotel disco on a Friday night and also into town as some bars were hang outs for mods.

I would not go to any clubs as there was always trouble including racial violence. For anyone not familiar with Liverpool, going to town was going into Liverpool city centre

We once rode up to the newly opened Wigan Casino for the all-nighter but after a few hours left and drove home.

There were several scooter gangs around at the time the biggest being Cloud another Tiger Bay in Orrell and Tamla Motown based in Formby but we would all come together to ride to Southport and Rhyl.

Once I returned home from work and it was too late to set off for Rhyl on the Friday night so along with two friends we set off first thing Saturday morning. We got as far as the junction with Queensferry when scooters were passing us heading back.

A lad on a Vespa pulled over and told us that Hells Angels were waiting for them.

We found out a day later that one of our friends was knocked off his scooter by the chasing horde and was struck on the side of his helmet with a bicycle chain and a cog on the end. He was in hospital for weeks, his scooter had about fifty mirrors and crash bars it looked great but had slowed him down.

My scooter also looked great but could shift as my friend Ste had geared it up to that of a 200cc it had to have a motorbike exhaust and other modifications such was the speed it built up and I had front and back carriers a back rest with a coach wheel trim and mirrors and flags.

My father knew a mechanic at Courtaulds who came to Speed kings in Rice Lane to check over the scooter before I bought it and would give me lessons to enable me to ride it.

Once me and Lesley were invited by her sister Edna and her husband Ronnie to Courtaulds club. My father did not know I was attending and said to Ronnie

'Why have you brought him here, you know whom I'm with'

I had to watch as my father was dancing cheek to cheek with a young blond female and as he was the compare at the club he was on the stage and delivered an embarrassing finger down the throat job

'This next song is especially for someone here tonight that is very special to me' turning to Lesley I said 'Well he isn't referring to me'

103

Then he proceeded to sing Gladys knight 'help me make it through the night' I just shook my head and went and sat down at the table. I did not arrive home till about 01.00AM the following morning having gone back to Lesley's after we left Courtaulds club.

My mother was waiting up and was screaming about the time and had also left several messages at Courtaulds for my father who rolled up about 02.00PM not at all pleased having had calls left for him.

My father launched a physical attack on me which sent my mother running into the square shouting at the top of her voice' listen everybody to my husband and son fighting'

My father let go of me having held me in a throat hold and said 'Fuckin get her in'

After bringing my mother in my dad cleared off in his car to return a few days later but not before saying to me that the blond he was with all night was the wife of the mechanic who taught me to ride my scooter which I knew to be untrue.

Before meeting Lesley, I had a few girlfriends but every time any would come the house my father if home would appear at the door and stand there asking them their names and what did they want with me. My mother would often take herself off to my Grandads but he moved up to Skelmersdale and she was more or less on her own, her so called close friend had emigrated.

The leaving of Liverpool

Then out of the blue just before I was 18 my mother decided to move to Skelmersdale, more about this later. I was leaving Ford and my best friends behind and only learnt of their fate many years later and Im the sole survivor.

The film 'Stand by me' one of the great coming of age films about a group of friends has a line at the end

'I never had any friends later on like the ones I had when I was twelve, Jesus, does anyone'?

That line in the film hits home and I feel somber just thinking about it.

Financial problems

I believe that the families money troubles affected how my mother treated all money including mine.

When I got my first weeks wages she said to me 'normally you are allowed to keep all your wages but you can start paying me your keep now'

She took £5.00 out of my £14.00 wages followed by 50p for a neighbours catalogue that I got a suit out of and another £1.00 pocket money for my two sisters.

My mother further insisted that I deliver the unopened wage packet to her each week. I had been saving my paper round money and had bought a six-gear racing bike to go from Ford to Maghull each day for work and when I bought my Lambretta scooter I advertised my bike for £5.00. My mother instructed me to take the bike to one of work friends that lived a few miles away and to give the bike to her friend's son, all free of course.

My mother once told a friend of hers that I would paint the entire inside of their home which I did, even getting the paint from work. I painted the house top to bottom and at the end of the job her friend said 'Thank you it is lovely and your mum said you are not charging us'

The final straw came when my mother turned up at our home with a work colleague to show her my artexing design such as fan and bark of a tree.

Her colleague said 'oh I love this' and 'I will have my living room ceiling done in the fan and all my walls in the bark of a tree'

My mother said 'all you need is to get is the artex' turning to me 'or can you get it' and I replied

'No, I cannot get bags of artex' and I then added 'I will need to come and see your house to give you a price'

The woman then replied 'oh I will have to leave it '

My mother took her friend to the door then returned wagging her finger saying 'you have embarrassed me, I told Linda you would do it free as a favour'

My youngest sister Joan did not know have to live through the years of hardship and my mother would say to my children 'You can't have those drinks or those chocolates they are Joan's'.

On the one and only occasion that I asked her if she could lend us £5.00 till I got paid as we had no food she said to Lesley
'You will have to come the shops with me and I will see what I have leftover'
After she had bought cans of coke and various biscuits for my sister Joan she handed Lesley £2.00 saying
'That is all I have and I want it back as soon as he gets paid'.
Once when I was unemployed my father said that I received too much unemployment benefit because I could afford to rent a twin tub washing machine at £2.00 per week suggesting we wash our clothes by hand in the river Tawd.
We had bought a front-loading washing machine from a catalogue and it stopped working after about a year and we could not afford a new one so we rented a second-hand twin tub.
We were certainly scammed as the person that we rented the machine off had looked at the front loader and declared it was beyond repair saying
'it is what we call in the trade, the fieldlings and they are gone' and 'I will get rid of it for you and give you one free week's rental on the twin tub'
How stupid can one be to be so easily taken in but I guess through a combination of innocence and ignorance why would we not accept the findings of a washing machine technician.
We had to take out a loan for Christmas presents for our children from a company called 'sturdy finance' not to be confused with any so named today.
This company that came from Upholland would offer £50.00 loans with added Interest of £15.00 and weekly repayment of £5.00 per week. Because we received the loan just before Christmas you would have the first week's payment deducted and then as there would be no collection till mid-January a further £10.00 would be deducted leaving you with £35.00 and still the £50.00 borrowed to repay.
I managed one week's payment then struggled as the rent was also £5.00 per week.
I would pull the curtain across the front door and turned the television off so when the doorstep collector called we would appear to be out and he would shout through the letter box
'I know you are in, your neighbours told me'

A wholly unlawful collection practice and quite common place then and I dare say now and I use that example when delivering 'Debt and Mental health training'. I also refer to how people prioritise one debt over another and keep the Provident or catalogue debt to enable future credit to be obtained for Christmas or replacement of white goods.

I fully understand and have empathy with people who have to do this and we should be supporting people to access credit unions to end the reliance on other forms of credit. We once received a debt letter from a company acting for Provident, it transpired that though we had made every payment the collector was pocketing the monies and was eventually prosecuted.

Back to college

I once rode my scooter to college but it stood out like a sore thumb surrounded by motorbikes. Another mod advised me against riding it to college saying that 'the hairies will take a screw driver to' it so I aired on the side of caution and commuted. He was probably correct because the older hairy students would make comments to us about our dress code being Fred Perry t-shirts, white cricket pants and parkas and riding hairdryers.

I saw very little of my best friends during my time in college and as an apprentice but would meet up with them on a Friday night to go to the Park Hotel disco.

Taking a short cut across the golf course, we would reminisce of the days of our child hood and the dredging of the golf course.

Ged reminded me of the time in Holy Ghost primary school when he climbed through a gap in the perimeter fence one lunch hour and in heavy fog returning about half an hour later with a number of golf hole red flags.

I don't recall asking why at the time, all I know was that the teachers were non-too pleased having to return the flags to the club house.

I think said Ged 'it was a funny thing to do at the time'

We would all meet up to go the match and occasional away games which were often amusing. We were once on a coach to Stoke and a young lad of 10 got on the coach, the driver shouted 'aye who is with this boy I need the money for his seat' he had of course bunked on the coach and was ejected.

There was a lot of football violence and rival gangs would unite at football matches putting their territorial disputes behind them on match days.

There was also fighting between Skinheads, Mods and greasers. We were all just teenagers, the greasers were adults some in their late twenties which was the case with the Hells Angels chapter from Crosby. They would drive around with impunity and wearing German helmets and sporting swastikas on their jackets. One night a bike with a side car and bath on it pulled up at the side of the chippie in Carr Meadow hey. One guy remained sat in the bath while the enormous giant of a rider pushed past us into the chippie followed by his girlfriend the pillion passenger who directed obscenities at us. Similarly, insulting Ged as he stood in the chippie queue who without hesitation let rip with his own insults.The giant turned to Ged and said 'you dare insult my old lady' moments later Ged and the giant were crashing through the plate glass window of the chippie. The guy in the side car bath jumped up but Jimmy landed him a punch sending him back into the side car. Before long a police black Mariah van arrived, the Hells Angels left on their bike and Ged having decided to remain was pointed out and hurled into the back of the police van.

We watched as he was driven away waving to us from the back of the police van, with Ronnie remonstrating with the police 'He has my chippie money, can't you just get it off him'

That was how it was, you never knew what the night would bring and we decided to stop congregating at the shops it just wasn't safe. Once a black hackney pulled up and about six guys jumped out with one waving an axe above his head. This same individual later stabbed a young woman with a knitting needle after she spurned his advances and he was locked up for a few years.

I once got into an altercation at Cookson's pub when four of us decided to have a pint in there before going to meet some friends in the Cabbage Inn. We had only been sat a few minutes when two couples in their thirties came in.

The two men were dressed in teddy boy clothing with DA haircuts and one of the females said 'These are our seats'

Barry picked up his chair to exam the underneath

'No, I don't see any names on this chair'

Ronnie said 'come on let's go' the other female chewing bubble gum, blew a big bubble at Barry who called her a 'disgusting mongrel' One of the teddy boys who held a past reputation told us in no uncertain terms what he was about to do to us.

The barman Frank said 'come on take this outside' and we filed out. There followed a spectacle that is worth telling just for this alone. The teddy boy with the reputation started hopping from one foot to another saying 'You dancing, were dancing' He then put his hand in his drape jacket and pulled out a steel comb and started to comb his quiff back whilst still hopping from foot to foot.'Fuck this' I said catching him off guard landing a punch under his chin sending him backwards onto the cobbles and not getting up. The other teddy boy just put his arms up in a I'm not getting involved gesture so we walked off towards the Cabbage Inn to the sounds of the two girls shouting abuse and threats.

Needless to say, I gave Cookson's a wide berth after that.

There were several violent incidents one night which culminated in my being attacked and badly beaten. I arrived home late after day release at college and decided to go the chippie. I considered driving around on my scooter but decided to walk instead.

It was eerily quiet on the estate and I was wondering what was up as no one was around at all when suddenly I heard someone shout

'Aye' on turning I seen two guys and next minute a brick was coming towards me.

I fell to the floor and moments later heard motorbikes pulling up. I could see heavy motor bike boots as they came towards my face and I tried to roll into a ball while hurling abuse at my assailants. Then suddenly the main attack was over and I lay still for about 10 minutes while still receiving the odd kicking as other attackers ran past. I got to my feet and though I did not feel any pain during the attack I became aware of a wet warmth running down by face and neck and I was struggling to breathe and walked to my house. To cut a long story short I had been stabbed in the back which was later reported to have been with a meat hook There were two holes in my parka but only one had gone through into my back puncturing a lung.

I had a head injury and cuts and abrasions all over my face and torso and a couple of broken ribs. No one was ever charge for the attack on me or the violent attacks that occurred earlier in the evening with one person slashed across he torso with a carpet knife and another person hit over the head with a bottle at Cookson's bridge.

I use to enjoy going to away matches, they were akin to the Jolly boys outing in only fools and horses but I ceased to go after my first and only visit to Old Trafford. Three football specials left Lime street with the expectation that each train would await the next trains arrivals and we would all make our way to the ground, safety in numbers. Just before we pulled into Victoria station the train windows were shattered with bricks a precursor of what was to come.

Exiting Victoria station there were no Reds fans at all from the two earlier trains they had all been sent off to the ground but we still felt relatively safe there being quite a number of us.

On arriving at the ground, I entered the scoreboard away supporters end and had only just got inside when I heard 'scouse bastard' and there were several Man Utd supporters surrounding me.

I seemed to be alone and realised that they had read the label on my jeans Flemings County Road Walton Liverpool 4 so I made for the turn style were another Liverpool supporter who I recognised from Bootle technical college shoved me through the turn style.

He also shoved another supporter through whilst he was being punched about the face and body.

The stewards inside that end did nothing and we watched as other supporters some bleeding similarly climbed out of the turn styles.

I would say that the ground had emptied of Liverpool supporters by half time and you could have filled just one train going back to Lime street not three.

On our way back to Victoria station there was sporadic violence and we were glad to get to the station but later that afternoon we heard an almighty roar of 'UTD' as hundreds of UTD fans poured into Victoria station but the police kept them at bay.

The church warden

I mentioned earlier in the book on how the church warden would try to catch us on each and every occasion he seen us in the cemetery and that was never lost on us. At 17 years of age we went to Christmas eve mass in the old chapel in Ford cemetery and the church warden having not forgotten us said very much to our annoyance 'Behave yourself in church'

'Fuck off' said Ste turning to us and saying 'Who the fuck does he think he is'

Ste then disappeared outside and appeared midway through the service.

'Where have you been' I asked 'Had some work to do'

Puzzled I shook my head and let it go in one ear out the other. However, Ste being a trainee mechanic carried some tools with him all the time 'just in case we need anything' he would say.

He decided to completely strip the engine on the church wardens 50cc moped leaving the engine parts screws and all neatly laid out on the floor. And so, the last act of the six plus years war with the church warden was played out.

My last Christmas with my friends

We spent Christmas in Geds listening to John Lennon 'war is over' and David Bowie Changes and Aladdin Sane, the tracks 'John I'm only dancing' 'Drive in Saturday' and Changes my all-time Bowie favourite' s and Life on Mars.

In between Christmas and New Years eve I found myself at a girl's house in Litherland then later went to the Ford lane chippie. I tapped on the door of a car to ask the time and a big hairy guy got out and said' Don't be banging on my car' and I was then flat out on the floor having being smacked under the chin.

I got up and hurled abuse at him which led to him getting out again but he was called back in by one of the others, giving me a finger motion before driving off.

My friends were aghast at my being at the Ford lane chippie alone Jimmy said 'Bobby what the fuck where you doing down there' Ged was all for going there but I talked him out of it.

That was my second unfortunate experience with alcohol over the Christmas of 1973.

The first was at the close of the Green park site for Christmas, most of the non-trades went to the Hare and Hounds in Maghull while the site agents and foremen went to the coach and Horses. I was plied with Pernod and pints of Skol lager and it was suggested that I go to the Coach and Horses to see Myles.

One of the labourers who was driving and on shandies told me to put on my bib and brace so Myles the bosses will think I have just finished work.

I was taken to the lounge of the Coach and Horses and pushed inside.

'Is that the apprentice from Green Park' I heard someone say, then the room was swirling around.

Next, I recall being dropped off at the railings on Cookson's bridge and spent the next day in bed.

Once we went to the Eden Vale in Netherton and on leaving we got on the canal bank and set off for Swifts lane bridge where we would part ways with some of our mates that lived in Daleacre Drive.

Ronnie had bought an Afghan coat that he proudly wore but no one could understand why he would purchase such a coat and not buy a sheepskin or Leather jacket instead and his saying 'I like it' and 'I'm not asking you to wear it' was lost on us.

Such was the ribbing that Ronnie took all night since appearing with the coat he took it off and threw it in the canal

'There are you all happy now, it's gone'

We burst into laughter at which Ronnie shouted

'Fuck you lot I'm getting it back' He then jumped into the canal to retrieve his coat. We pulled him and the coat out and a few days later we met him at the now gone Strand Park hotel and he was wearing the coat.

'Nice coat Ronnie where did you get if from' said Barry

'Is it waterproof' asked Ged

'Fuck off' came the reply

I met my girlfriend Lesley towards the end of January but my friends would continue to knock for me and say just leave seeing her for one night and come out with us but I was smitten hook line and sinker. I had seen Lesley on Pendle drive when I was over there on my scooter. She was with a small group and though we looked at each other it would be a few nights before we dated.

My friend Barry came around one night and unknown to me Lesley had bumped into Barry weeks earlier.

'Do you know him' she asked

'Yes, he is one of my best friends'

She then told me that she was with some friends and whatever had occurred Barry wanted to fight them all and said he would throw them in the canal.

I laughed but inside I knew he would have carried out the threat.

Before I met lesley me, Barry and Jimmy were in the Strand Park hotel and an older group of troggs came in.

Barry took a liking to one of the females and could not keep his eyes off her.

After about half an hour one of the troggs came over and said Barry was 'making the chicks feel uncomfortable' at which Barry laughed and said

'Which is the chick you all look the same with your long hair'

Before we could suggest the trogg return to his friends Barry stood up and was about to pour his pint over the guy's head when another trogg intervened and said

'Hey no need man we have grass and booze at our pad'

Me and Jimmy declined the offer as we were going to the Park hotel but Barry left with them.

Barry would resurface the following night telling us the wildest of tales that cannot be printed of his night of debauchery in the pad in Field lane.

I would add that Barry was not afraid of anything and going on his own with them was no problem for him nor us.

Thinking back to those days me and Jimmy went to the annual Litherland gala that took place on Litherland Moss lane playing fields. The gala would have a fun fare and on the third day during the early 70s there would be an arranged fight between Netherton and Dodge against Litherland and Seaforth and they were quite bloody affairs.

Me and Jimmy decided to get away from the field before it all kicked off and headed over towards the gala tent were there was a lama tied up against a post.

Jimmy decided it would make an unusual pet so he unhooked the rope and off we went out the gate and headed towards the 'ghostie' the cinder path alongside Litherland high school.

No one challenged us they just looked at us, and a few asked
'Is that a lama' and Jimmy would reply
'No, it's a cross between a great Dane and an Irish wolf hound it
got its neck stretched in the railings so I'm taking it the vet'
We came out the cinder path at Sterrix lane and there was a police
officer searching lads going into the fair and on hearing the
laughter he turned and looked over at us.
With a puzzled look on his face, he stopped searching the lads
and went onto his radio so we tied the lama to school railings and
fled.

Holy Ghost club
The Holy Ghost club introduced a weekly disco for local
teenagers so I rode up on my scooter parked outside and paid the
entrance fee. There were a number of scooters outside one being
my friend Tony from school who had brought me in his mother's
coffee cream cake. I had only been in the disco about 10 minutes
when a fight broke out between.
Yes, you guessed it Ged and Barry who were scrapping like hell
right in front of the DJ who stopped playing and was trying to
move his speakers.
I went forward and dragged Ged and Barry apart and they
proceeded to give me hug when two staff came over and started
to throw us out. I protested my innocence to no avail and was
ejected along with Ged and Barry who were now laughing and
calling for the staff to fight them. They then decided to go to the
Park Hotel and I said I will take my scooter home first and see
them there and off they went cutting across the golf course.
I had just pulled at my house and was getting off my scooter when
Lesley showed up asking if I had seen her friend, well she had to
say something.
I said I hadn't and asked her if she wanted to come in and that
was how we met. We would go to see lots of films 'A clockwork
orange' on the Albany in Maghull now a Lidl supermarket. The
Exodus on the ABC in Lime street we queued up for hours on the
Friday, the queue spreading around the block and had to return
the following day which we did early enough to be first in the
queue.

I swear that film was and still is the most frightening film I have ever seen.

We would go to the Futurist in Lime street, watch one film then across to the ABC to see 'The Dirty Dozen'

Lesley was a laboratory assistant at Hewson & Hardwicke's in Pall Mall and I would be on day release from work on a Friday at Bootle Technical college and meet her at exchange station.

We would go for walks taking our family dog Rebel a long-haired German shepherd out along Lunt.

I would tell her of the exploits of me and my friends and as I write this book she says I remember you telling me about that.

Once we drove to Southport and I was surrounded by motorbikes and greasers in a car and ordered to 'get you and your bean can out of our town' another remarked that 'It was just as well I had a chick with me' two of them followed us down the coast road as far as Toad hall in Ainsdale then turned back just like the scene in Rambo where the police escort him to the city limits.

I even stopped going to the match and we would spend Saturday's shopping around Walton Vale which was a great shopping place then.

We would go into my favourite record shop Allen Bros on Moss Lane as you could get any record in there including import soul records not yet in the UK charts but played on radio Luxembourg.

When Lesley first took me to her home in Thornton I was taken aback by how she could just go into the fridge and help herself.

Her father Harry an ex-merchant service cook made the most incredible beef burgers and pasties and Lesley picked up his cooking skills.

He would say 'does he not get fed' and of course he was not far wrong. Lesley's father passed away at just 61 years of age he had emphysema having never fully recovered from the war.

He was torpedoed twice in the Atlantic and once in the Malta convoy and spent days floating in a raft and told me of the absolute terror of the German stuka dive bombers.

Lesley had a few uncles one being her uncle Norman who we were very close to and I was one of the last people to see him before he passed away as he had been admitted to Aintree hospital and I was fortunate to be working for MIND at the hospital and could see Norman outside of visiting hours.

He was another brave man and stormed the beaches at Normandy at just 18 years of age and was subsequently wounded in Caen. He said he rounded a corner and ran right into a German soldier who took aim at him and shot him in the legs. Norman said either he was a very poor shot or must have had enough of bloodshed. He said whilst on the beach at Normandy he lay down next to another soldier who had a cigarette in his mouth but was dead having been shot in the forehead.

Norman was a fanatical Liverpool fan and I arranged a trip for the community of Captains Green to visit Liverpool's ground and museum and I took uncle Norman and he said It was 'one of the best days ever'

I also took a coach to Everton ground as the secretary of the newly formed Captains Green Community Association which I formed along with Anne-Heywood Lloyd who asked me if I minded working with her because she was a conservative voter and also Flo Taylor who was instrumental in setting up the Home Watch scheme before the community association.

I resigned as secretary of association when I became a councillor. Lesley had another relative her auntie Lizzie who lived in Seaforth who initially referred to me as not only a 'Catholic get' but also a 'Bootle buck' we later moved in with her and she treated us like were her own. Lizzie would go to Southport every 12 July to watch the orange lodge parade and would often make derogatory comments about Catholics and Lesley would remind her I was a catholic but it never bothered me I would just laugh at it all.

When I lived at home I would be embarrassed when Lesley came as when I asked if I could make us both a cup of tea my mother would reply 'use one tea bag' so I would be dunking the tea bag in and out of both cups.

'Can I make me and Lesley a round of toast?'

'one round you can have half a piece between you'

it was utterly shameful?

We would go to Allison club and watch different acts including the Chilites and life was wonderful then in September 1974 my mother dropped the bombshell

'We are moving to Skelmersdale next week and there is nowhere to leave your bike' meaning of course my Lambretta scooter.

My mother had done a house exchange and I knew nothing of it, I knew she had gone up to Skelmersdale but assumed it was to visit my granddad but she was also exchanging houses. My father had by this time gone to work in Leeds and was not supposed to be moving into the house in Skelmersdale but did return and used it as bolt hole.

The house my mother moved into and eventually bought was an end of terrace with the front door opening onto the street and no back entrance as she was on a hill.

My mother suggested that I leave my scooter at my grandads about a mile away which was not feasible and so I hastily tried to sell it even though I still had two years higher purchase payments to make.

A former school friend offered me £50 that I reluctantly accepted and over 10 years later Lesley went to work in a butcher shop in Walton to cover one day and the lad who had bought my scooter worked there and he informed Lesley that he crashed the scooter and it was written off, my prized SX Lambretta scooter registration ULV 89H

Having no way to travel from Skelmersdale to see Lesley, she asked her parents if she could move to Skelmersdale with us and they agreed which must have been heart rendering for them. There was no way that I could live in Lesley home as it was a two-bedroom flat and she shared a bedroom with her sister Moira. My mother met with Lesley mother and it was agreed for Lesley to come and live with the family and that Lesley would not have to pay any keep but at the end of the first week that Lesley stayed my mother demanded £10 off me which was double I had been giving. When I asked why she replied 'that girl cannot expect to stay for free' I reminded her what she had said about not taking keep off Lesley and she replied

'I'm not taking it off her I'm taking it off you'

The house that my mother exchanged with is in Eversley Tanhouse and had been painted in the most bizarre psychedelic fashion that I spent evenings after work and weekends trying to paint over.

Me and Lesley would meet at the ribble bus station at Skelhorne street and take the hours journey to Skelmersdale on the number 245 and be met with a meagre meal of a few breakfast chops and some chips.

Each morning my mother would abruptly march us onto the bus to work and one morning we were at the back of the bus queue and my mother struggled to force us on board and scowled and pointed her finger at us from the bus window as it drove away without us. We decided to take the day off work and went and bought what was the equivalent of a large full English breakfast times two and went back to my mother's to cook it and have a decent meal.

When we got back my sister Joan was still at the house and we bribed her with breakfast to keep quiet about us being there. My father having decided to return to the family home turned his attention to Lesley but I was not surprised at all and I knew I would be wasting my time telling my mother. Though I was furious I worried of the repercussions if I did tell her.

One Monday morning my father was leaving for Leeds and he grabbed me by the throat saying

'When I get back here on Friday I want you gone, that girl can stay but not you'

I wanted to say your deluded if you think she will stay here but decided against it so as not to incense him further.

We had to take the Monday off work and registered with a private rental company 'Bold street' rentals and paid £5 to a guy that resembled Michael Crawford. He would give us a list of houses to rent in Kensington and Newsham park and allover Queens Drive and we would spend at least an hour going to properties to be told sorry it has gone.

It was now getting near to the weekend and so at the end of October just a few weeks after moving to Skelmersdale me and Lesley left and having nowhere to go we went to her aunt Lizzie in Alexander house in Seaforth and as it was two bedroom we moved in unknown to Lesley parents.

Lizzie being sworn to secrecy and being paid keep never told anyone we were there and shamefully we kept up the pretense calling to Lesley's parents each Friday to see them before allegedly setting off for Skelmersdale.

I still had the £50 from my scooter sale and Coney fur coats were all the fashion so I bought Lesley one at a cost of £50 and some days she would leave it in the wardrobe in Lizzies.

One Friday night we went to Lesley's parents to see them before as usual catching the bus to Skelmersdale.

As we were about to leave Lesley's mother told us that she and Lesley older sister had gone to Lizzies flat to look for something of her uncles whose flat it originally was and lo and behold there was Lesley's Coney fur coat hanging up in the wardrobe so we had to come clean and apologised.

Lesley parents being aware of my father's behaviour understood but suggested we got married and it was the right thing to do as a few weeks later Lesley found out that she was pregnant and carrying our first daughter Clare.

We got married on 14 December 1974. the night before Lesley went to St William of York club with her older sister Edna and both her parents. It was arranged for me to meet my father and Mike Pilling and my sisters then boyfriend Peter and I reluctantly attended.

After just one drink I left to meet Lesley in the William of York as my father had started regaling us of his conquests notably my mother's so called best friend and his regaling contained extremely explicit accounts that sickened me.

Mike told me to go and told my father that he was out of order but on leaving my father suggested they all go with me. Later that evening Lesley's father told my father in no uncertain terms what he thought of his treatment of me. Lesley had an older brother Harry who died a few years earlier having suffered a coronary thrombosis attack and fell from a scaffold aged just 37.

The following night my mother had arranged a small party in her house that me Lesley and her mother travelled up for and my grandad and June and Mike and Sarah were there and it was okay till my father turned up.

We thought he had gone back to Leeds as he was not at our registry office wedding on the Saturday morning just Mike and Peter.

Once he came in the atmosphere changed and my grandad, June, Mike and Sarah all left and the party ended with my dad playing solitaire with a packet of cards.

We would buy crockery from Danny's stores in Mount Pleasant Waterloo and Paddy's market in Great Homer street as we were now looking for a house.

One morning in April Lizzie announced that she had been offered a one bedroom flat in Style Hey Thornton close to Lesley's mother and had accepted meaning me and Lesley were about to be homeless and we could not get local authority housing.

My grandad and his neighbour Charlie from the trade's council helped get us a house on the same estate as my grandads in Skelmersdale and a few doors away from Mike and Sarah and June's other son Robert and his wife who lived on the next terrace.

I was transferred to the new Norwest Holst housing development at Spencers lane. The site agents had worked in Maghull including the one who had taken the tins of paint. He was a dyed in the wool, Daily Mail reading tory voter who despised trade unions. Once when I got a pay rise on my birthday he said to me' big wage for you this week'

Followed by 'it's my son's birthday I don't get paid till next week, I don't suppose you could you lend some money so I can buy him a shirt'

I was not wishing to lend it but felt obliged and asked 'how much?' and he replied 'a fiver will do' needless to say he never paid the money back.

A few weeks later someone that lived by me was selling cheap sausage and bacon along with black pudding and I went into the site hut and asked if anyone wanted to order any and the same site agent said to me

'Get a few pounds each of bacon and sausage and a whole black pudding'

Adding

'Eggs if they are selling them if not fetch in half a dozen and we will sort you out '

I told him it has to be cash up front and he said

'I have just said we will sort you out' came his curt reply

I never did and he pulled me a week later

'Hey where's the sausage and bacon' I told him I could not get it and he went into the site and said

'That tight arsed little fuck won't get you lads any sausage and bacon' I wanted to remind him of the £5.00 he borrowed but it would have been a total waste of my time.

A few months later and still an apprentice I became the youngest federation steward for UCATT and was approached by the same site agent who said

'Hey Fuckie what are you trying to do to the site?'

Norwest had brought in lumpers to finish the painting and I got UCATT involved and as there was no steward I became it.

I had no real interest in trade unionism and was more interested in peoples war stories. I was a Territorial army trooper with The Duke of Lancaster's own Yeomanry in Wigan before joining the Royal Marine Reserve at Morpeth dock in Birkenhead. However, when I had started as an apprentice my foreman Myles suggested that I join the union and described them as a 'necessary evil'.

Two managers from Norwest Holst came to the site and along with the site agent entered the house that I was painting and quite menacingly demanded the names of all the activists in the Skelmersdale trade's council and local UCATT branch. Unknown to me then Norwest Holst were signatories to the Economic league that held a black list of builders.

I reported the demand for names to the UCATT central office and Jimmy Cousins one of the regional organisers attended the site and was appalled at the lack of safety and got the factory inspectorate involved and so the lumpers never got a foothold. I was not long after sent across to Pensby and as far afield as Poulton le Fylde and Penwortham and no other worker on the site spoke up.

Once whilst at Spencers lane I was finishing the treads and rises on the stairs being the last job to do when the front door burst open and a labourer who resembled Compo of the last of the summer wine pushed past me shouting 'out the way' running up the stairs straight into the toilet to be followed almost immediately by the unmistakable sound of him emptying his bowels and groans of relief.

As it was raining heavily there was mud splashes all over the magnolia walls on the stairwell and dirty boot marks mixed with white gloss paint all the way up the stairs and into the toilet.

The labourer came out saying 'I Fucking needed that'

I said 'Look at the state of my paintwork its ruined'
'Oh, you just need to rub it down and dab the walls'
I said 'How the hell can I rub it down its bloody wet gloss'
Out he went and I started to clean off the stairs with white spirits when the site foreman walked in.
'This finished yet Fuckie'
I told him it would have been till naming the labourer burst in.
His reply was 'tough'
Followed by
'You will just have to stay late to finish it, it gets fucking handed over tomorrow' or your wages are docked
After it had turned 16.30PM the site was empty, the foreman being dropped off at his drinking hole. The labourers would collect him of a morning and he would be stinking of alcohol and in the same clothes and that evidently was where my £5.00 had gone.
As I was just leaving I noticed the labourer who had burst into the house had laid a quarry tile step and had placed a plank across it to the door.
I went across removed the plank and jumped up and down on the steps collapsing the tiles then went home.
My father rolled up unexpectedly one morning and asked me to come out for a drink. I informed him I could not afford to come out and his reply was 'I never asked if you had money' I did not really want to go for a drink but once again I reluctantly went along and was sat with my sister Joan and her friends and after about two drinks he loudly asked whose round of drinks was it.
Turning to me he said 'it is your round isn't it' I wanted the ground to swallow me up and said 'I had no money' his response was to say
'Well why did you come out then' I felt totally humiliated as everyone thought it was quite amusing
I did not associate much with my father again for about 8 years though he would periodically request if I could get him military insignia like parachute wings and commando flashes allegedly for his boss's son which I did but only though I guess he would never have said how he acquired them.

We were really struggling financially being on apprentice wages and we could not afford to pay for the oil-fired central heating which only covered the downstairs of the property.

We purchased two paraffin heaters one for the living room and one for the kitchen -dining room. The heaters gave off really good heat but scorched the carpet underneath and added to the condensation and black mould that would appear. Nevertheless, we had no choice than to keep using them until the fuel was changed from oil to gas and we had the heating put back on but we were still indebted for a large oil bill.

The paraffin would last us about a week and I would walk the two miles to the petrol station that sold the paraffin taking a large plastic container in our daughters' buggy to fill up.

A couple of times the paraffin had not came in so I would have to return a few hours later, I can still smell that paraffin now as I write.

When I joined the labour party in 1983 there were other ex-forces members and we had several heated arguments with members of the 'troops out movement' opposed to British troops in Northern Ireland.

There were many solidarity support groups such as Chile and Nicaragua and Solidarnosc all of which got full support but not so for Palestine even though the Labour Middle East council were supporting the right to self-determination and a Palestine homeland and I could never understand the hostility that existed and being knew to all of this would ask

'Why cannot both peoples co-exist'

The ward party was also affiliated to the Campaign for Nuclear Disarmament (CND) and a fund raiser was held in the home of an activist who had spent weeks at Greenham Common.

The fund raiser was invaded by supporters of the far right in what was clearly an organised invasion.

Despite calls to 999 it took around 45 minutes for the police to arrive and then it was just a male sergeant and one young female officer. Within a week or so the local branch of CND closed down after what I was told were 'special branch' confiscations of the local CND branch members records.

It is interesting to note that none of the far-right wing supporters were ever investigated regarding the home invasion despite their names being known. I often wonder are these the same 'dark forces at work in Britain' that our late monarch Queen Elizabeth II referred. That said I'm very much a royalist and swore allegiance to her majesty the queen and all her heirs and successors notwithstanding the conduct of some of the royals. I became more aware of the let's say 'the men in black' when I applied for a position at the atomic weapons establishment in Aldermaston some years later, a position that I was successful in procuring.

I travelled down to Hampshire on the train taking about eight hours from Lime street to Basingstoke then a bus to Tadley in Berkshire where I stayed in the MOD hostel. There was no channel 4 on the television and I palled up with another ex-serviceman who had been at the Faslane nuclear submarine base. There was the usual 'why have you came down here for jobs?' and we would respond accordingly 'The job advert said come and live and work in beautiful Berkshire so here we are'

The successful candidates would eventually be afforded housing in Reading or Andover but that would not be for at least six months and regular weekend travel home was out of the question. The last train from Basingstoke on the Friday left at 18.00PM arriving in Lime street at midnight and you had to get the 08.00 train back on the Sunday morning.

When we went for our interviews I was asked 'are you or have you ever been a member of any political party?' which they likely already knew. To join the Royal Marines Reserve I was screened by naval intelligence for six weeks even with references I had from police officers so I guessed the MOD would similarly have screened me.

I told them I was a member of the Labour party and one interviewer laughed saying

'We asked are you or have you ever been a member of a political party'

I met up with the lad from Scotland later and we discussed how we thought we did and I said 'I think I did okay' he said 'I don't think the money is that great, but beats being unemployed' he then commented on the interview panel and secret service etc.

I had gone into a cubicle and he was at the sink and when I came out I caught a glimpse of a man in a suit standing back against the wall clearly listening to the conversation.

Once he knew that I had seen him he went and I said 'some guy in a suit was stood back listening to our conversation' and he replied 'that is me fucked then'

I was invited back for a further interview and offered the position and I asked   if the Scottish lad was successful and one of the interviewers revealed that he had not been.

Back to Skelmersdale

There were 400,000 building workers on the dole nationally and any work in Skelmersdale was short term such as painting a single housing estate. Once that estate had ended you would struggle to work again as the firms were reluctant to take Skelmersdale workers with them to other jobs outside of the town because of what they viewed as militancy. I acquired a job with Unit construction that lasted about twelve weeks and I worked with a painter called Bill who came from London and lived on the same estate as me and we became great friends and had many humorous moments.

There was a strict 'no rollers' to be used on the walls and ceilings only on the doors that had to be feathered off with a brush. It was nigh impossible to make any bonus so Bill brought in a sheepskin roller and tray and we would lock the front door and roll the walls and ceilings then brush over them to remove any signs that we had used a roller. Once we were rolling the walls and we had the radio on loud so as to excuse us not hearing the foreman knocking on the door. The foreman was very much akin to Nimrod in the builder bible 'The Ragged Trousered Philanthropist' placed a ladder up against the window and we turned to see him snarling through at us and from that day on we had to await his daily inspection before we could continue.

 He would often leave us sitting doing nothing for hours then appear.

We did make a bonus when he was on his two weeks holiday and that infuriated him even more on his return as he knew we would have returned to the roller and when the estate was finished me and Bill were made redundant.

I got another job with a firm called Sharrock's that my uncle Peter was also working for and I had not seen him for many years till then but a few months later Peter left to work for a new company called Paintaway. He asked me to join him but I stayed on the site in Skelmersdale with Sharrock's but would work with Peter again in the coming years.

After the Skelmersdale job finished I was sent to work on an estate by Gillmoss bus garages and there was a clerk of works called Cliff who knew every trick in the book.

The rates for the houses were okay once you started the painting but the money for the preparation was virtually non- existent. You would be given an entire terrace and it involved burning off all the flaking paintwork to nearly every window then primed them but first you had to clean out all the gutters.

I climbed up the ladder to remove clumps of grass and was aghast as the whole of the guttering needed cleaning out so I removed a section of noticeable grass either side of the large bedroom window and started to burn off the paintwork when Cliff appeared and said 'you done all them gutters, that was quick'

I got the ladders and placed them where I had removed the grass either side but to my horror he said

'I will tell you where to put the ladder' and with the gutters not being cleaned he ordered me to red lead every gutter it was of course my own fault.

I was then sent to work on a tower block but on getting into the cradle the person I was due to be working with declared he was scared of heights and I eventually left. Bill my colleague from Unit contacted me about a job with him as he was now working for a small contractor and Bill had been allocated one of the contractor's small fleet of vans.

The firm had a contract with Skelmersdale development corporation to paint houses before they re-let the houses. Sometimes we would go into homes that had olive green walls and ceilings which was basically mould.

The works sheet would say apply two coats of anti-condensation paint sometimes we would have to leave a heat lamp on in a room to dry out the walls so we could apply the paint.

'How the fuck are these people supposed to pay the electric bill for the lamp'

'Oh, they don't use much' would be the clerk of works reply.

There would be toddlers and despairing parents anxious to get out of the bloody place and we could offer nothing other than anti-condensation paint and our sympathy for their plight.

We were tasked with removing wood chip from one house in Digmoor that had been painted over with silk vinyl and would not come off no matter how much water was applied to it.

The firm purchased a steam wall paper remover as you only had two hours to complete that job then another hour to complete another etc.

The wall paper steamer did little to assist so Bill said 'We will just leave it on in the room while we go for lunch' which was 12.30PM to 1.00pm and so Bill dropped me off but he never returned till 02.15 as he had to take his cat to the vet.

We pulled up at the house to see the fire service at the house and the front door forced open.

The wall paper steamer had run out of water and went on fire and steam was everywhere, it was damaged beyond repair but the wall paper was all hanging off the walls.

One of the first things we did on getting to a void property was to look in the loft to see if there was anything in it worth selling. We would recover surf boards and items of furniture that we would take to a second-hand shop in Sandy lane and sell. The other staff would to refer to us as sick pigeons 'as we were always in the loft'

We would also take shrubs out of the gardens as we both loved gardening and once I dug up a seven-foot conifer that was tied to Bills roof rack and transported to mine at lunch time. On the way to my house Bill noticed the top of the red and white van of one of the firm's bosses coming along the other side of the dual carriageway which had a five-foot beech head that ran the entire length of the central reservation.

Bill was driving one of the fleets of blue vans and because of the hedge the boss could only see the top of the van with a conifer on its roof rack and it was also raining so mud was pouring down over the windows. Bill dropped me and the conifer off and went and got the van cleaned.

Later that afternoon everyone was summoned to the yard were the boss walked around puzzled inspecting each van before sending every one off.

Bill was not so lucky a few weeks later when he decided to take his partner up to Kirkby Lonsdale for the bank holiday weekend in the van of course. While sitting having a quiet drink at an inn he said 'suddenly I seen the bosses red and white van coming down the lane to the inn' and from that day onwards the vans had to go to the office on a Friday night for the mileage to be taken and re-taken on the following Monday morning.

I left and went to another job that lasted about six weeks then returned to work with Bill again which was easy as the firm could not get tradesmen as the wages were just 'flat cap' basic and not much more than people got in state benefit. Before returning to work with Bill I had worked on steel works on the Gillibrand's estate where you would have to stand on trap ends and use a striker that being a brush on the end of a pole to paint above a boiler.

The clerk would get a mirror to look behind the pipes in the toilet and you had to use a glove to run the paint behind the pipes. There was a contracts manager who had the same surname as a sea food retailer and one morning two of the painters were talking about what they were getting 'the dressed crabs are great' and 'I like the potted shrimps' Being of interest I asked and was told 'did you not know' naming the contracts manager 'that his family owned the sea food company' Not giving it a second thought, I awaited the arrival of the contracts manager a few days later and handed him my order. The look of anger on his face said it all 'is this what is called scouse humour' I stood there knowing that I had been done up like a kipper, no pun intended. Once he left there was an outburst of laughter from the other painters.

On returning to work with Bill we went to a house in Little Digmoor and the tenant came out and on leaving he said 'Erm do not open the door to the front room' I was incensed as we were only painting the walls and ceilings in the bathroom room and said 'what do we want to go in the front room for we are only doing the bathroom upstairs' he then apologised saying 'sorry I never meant to offend you'

128

I shrugged my head and said 'well you did' and he got in his car and left. Bill was carrying the step ladders up the stairs and I said 'I wonder why he said that about the front room door'

Bill replied 'beats me must have something in there he doesn't want anyone to see'

I decided to open the door to have a look, and on opening I seen a Jack Russel dog sat on an armchair. It started to growl and bare its teeth and then it sprung for the door which I just closed in time.

'Hey Bill it's a bleeding dog and vicious as fuck'

I then took a couple of tins up the stairs and on coming down decided to take another peek at the dog so the scene was repeated. When we had finished I was taking the cans back to the van and decided to have a final look and started to open the door.

The dog had got wise and was waiting behind the door and got its head out and it was snapping and snarling so I got to the front door as it started tearing away at the net curtain and shouted through the letter box.

'Bill the dogs got out'

The dog stopped tearing at the net curtain and hurtled up the stairs at Bill who threw at dust sheet over it and flung himself into the bedroom and slammed the door.

The dog was tearing hell out of the dust sheet and Bill had to hang out the bedroom window and drop into the garden nearly breaking his ankle in the process.

We sat in the van, Bill in pain waiting for the tenant to return and having to tell him that somehow the dog got out which he never believed.

A complaint was put in but as the only damage was to the net curtain and our dust sheet he was given £10 and an apology the £10 duly deducted from mine and Bills wages.

Eventually I went to work for a Preston company who were working on the Scott estate in Ormskirk and an older couple in one of the houses I worked on were wonderful and looked after me with breakfast and lunch. One day one of the other painters stole a scraper that belonged to them and though I had it returned there was to be no more hospitality. I was approached by the contract manager who said 'If you cause any union problems on here will have your legs broken'

He then turned and walked off jovially chatting to other painters. I was made redundant when the estate was finished albeit they had been awarded another contract locally. I was the only time served painter on that site all the others were from Preston and had been on government training schemes and it showed in many ways including time, quality and even their handling of paint brushes and ladders.

I took a temporary job in a factory shoving polystyrene into a grinder from 06.00AM till 06.00PM but I lasted just a week. The noise even with ear defenders was horrendous and a machine fitter noticing my discomfort said to me 'the trick is to shove a 40mm in with the 20mm and it will clog the machine and I won't get around to fixing it for a few hours' and so I did. There was a grinding noise and the machine stopped and I was given a brush and saw dust to throw around the machines and sweep up any oil and stuff. Having started brushing up I stopped and was taking to another worker when it came over the tannoy.

'Will the man who is temporary employed as a sheet grinder and who is temporary brushing up report to Mr Aspen (not his real name) in the office immediately'

This Mr Aspen had an office that overlooked the factory floor so off I went and climbed the stairs to his office and knocked on the door, no response so I knocked again and still no response. I was just about to knock a third time when just like a scene from 'The rise and fall of Reginald Perrin' were Reggie is summoned to CJs office I received the order

'Enter'

In I went to be addressed 'we are not employing you to stand idle gossiping'

All that was missing was 'I didn't get where I am today idle gossiping'

Out I went and I started brushing up again when a guy on a fork lift who seeing I was new asked me how I was doing adding that I must be crazy to do twelve hours shifts, when the tannoy opened up again

'Will the man who is temporary employed as a sheet grinder and who is temporary brushing up report to Mr Aspen in the office immediately'

So off I went and again the same knock on the door, wait, knock again wait then

'Enter'

In I walked and was again read the riot act. A few days later the grinder broke again but no at my hands and I was once again brushing up and stopped to chat when the tannoy sounded

'Will the man who is temporary employed as a sheet grinder and who is temporarily brushing up report to Mr Aspen in the office immediately'

It was now like a scene from the 'Great Escape' were Steve McQueen kept being returned to the cooler with his baseball and as I walked to the stairs leading up to the office the only thing missing was the tune from the bloody film, but this time I did not knock I opened the door marched in and said

'You know what you can do with your brush and your grinder' and I quit.

I decided to volunteer at the Skelmersdale Unemployed Workers Centre in Digmoor which was situated right adjacent to a chemist shop owned by the husband of the then Leader of Lancashire County Council.

The centre received no support from the Labour party as it was formed by members of the Trades council who all happened to be members of the Communist Party of Great Britain some of whom would join the Labour party in years to come. There was initial surprise at my offering to help being the only Labour party member to do so and I took a TUC welfare rights course and was providing free welfare rights advice. The centre was providing a service that was otherwise not being provided and yet because of them being communists they were repeatedly denied funding and relied on local trade union branches.

The centre supported the peoples march for jobs and had food cooperatives and provided free donated good quality clothing for families.

Around the same time in 1984 a South Sefton TUC unemployed centre was established in Waterloo but closed after financial irregularities came to light but it was not fraudulent just monies given or loaned to desperate people.

As a family we hoped to move back to Sefton in late 1984 we had been accepted by Sefton council and were looking forward to moving when we got a letter from Skelmersdale development saying they would not agree to our transfer as we had an outstanding oil central heating bill. I had no means whatsoever to pay the bill and walked dejected up to the unemployed centre in Digmoor.

As I was walking past a church the mother and aunt of one of the CND activists were coming out of the church and asked when I was moving and I told them it was not now happening because of the oil bill.

To my delight the aunt offered to lend me the money and to pay her back when I could.

I believe in fate and Karma and if I had not been passing that church at that very moment in time I would not have seen them.

On coming to Sefton, I was able to get some work a bit here a bit there.

Once I was working in Toxteth and was helping with repairs to a chimney stack when suddenly some men nicked the extension ladder and we were stuck on the roof for hours.

Another time I was not picked up from the job and had to walk home from Wavertree to Netherton Park lane estate some hike but no choice as I had no bus fare. I got work with my uncle Peter and we would be painting Ethel Austin shops all over the Northwest and Wales of a weekend and once we did a farm house In Cheshire that had several race horses. It was a huge farm house and required several coats of Sandtex masonry paint and each evening we had to wash using a tap at the stables. One day it was blazing hot and the owner and some friends sat drinking cocktails whilst watching us and eventually sent across a jug of cold water. There were again many humorous memories, we were renovating houses in Rocky Lane and you had to have a number two in an empty cement bag then toss it on the skip. There was a mongrel that kept coming around being fed by one of the labourers and the dog would jump up and lick his face every time it seen him. One day one of the young labourers who was nicknamed 'damage' for reasons that will soon become apparent had done a number two and tossed the bag on the skip.

With this being Monday and the dog likely not been fed since Friday it ran up the plank and tucked into the content of the bag.

We were balking watching when the labourer who fed the dog appeared out of one of the houses and the dog set off to greet his friend. Before we could say 'don't' he was on his knees while patting the dog as it licked his face.

A day later we heard a 'whoosh' and a big fountain of water shot into the air, damage had broken the main water supply pipe to the street.

We went to a now occupied house to touch up some doors on the ground floor that had to be planed the occupant leaving the key as she had to go to work.

While me and the Joiner were going about our work a labourer came in and was going on about the woman that lived in the house and then he went upstairs.

We shouted up 'what are you doing' and 'you better not rob anything'

A short while later the front door was opened with a key and in walked the female occupant's boyfriend who said he had come to collect something which may or not have been true.

He heard the noise upstairs but must have assumed it was someone doing work when suddenly the labourer came down the stairs and jumped out shouting 'De Der' sporting a pair of the woman's underwear on his head.

We just stood shocked not saying a word when the labourer turned to the woman's boyfriend and asked 'Who are you'

'Who the hell are you and why have you got my girlfriends underwear on your head' came the response

He did of course get sacked.

Sometimes you would go into a house to carry out touch up work and would be greeted with a five-pound note laying on the floor in the room you were going to work which ceased to surprise you.

I applied for work in the Isle of Man and was offered three different positions and opted for a firm called Cooke and Yates and they met me and Lesley at the airport and took us around several houses that were up for sale.

What we did not know at the time was that you could not purchase a home on the island through a building society only a bank and had to be resident on the island for six months.

We could only be offered holiday accommodation during the close season which was too much of a risk and despite the firm appealing to the Manx government to grant us key worker status it was declined. I could not work on the island and leave Lesley in Bootle as she was expecting our fourth child and the company tried everything to assist even featured an article in the Manx Independent it just did not make sense when there was a shortage of such skills on the island.

One morning we had a letter arrive from the island' it was simply addressed to Robert Brennan, Bootle but delivered and Inside was a simple message 'Stay away, too many of you here already' and signed Manxie. We were shocked given that my step nan June Pilling originated from the island and of course Lesley uncle had worked on the IOM steam packet boats.

The Manx Independent printed the letter and condemned the writer and though initially saddened at the loss of an opportunity my life would not have been as fulfilling if we had gone.

I was offered a position in Carlisle but Cumbria police told us to stay away from the area where we had been offered a house it was then an area with high levels of ASB and other crimes.

I would occasionally do sign writing and had once took an art class for a few hours at Delphside County primary school in Skelmersdale where a labour party colleague was a teacher and there being no art teacher. I'm quite good at still life and cartoon characters and would do art for fish mongers and Disney characters on demand and sign write door signs for people and once did a caricature of another councillor that ended up being passed around the council chamber.

Yet I was still applying for jobs and receiving no replies.

New Year's fucking Eve

A line from the opening scenes of the film 'No Surrender' about New Year's Eve in Liverpool and I make no apology for using the expletive as a headline.

I hated New Year's Eve, loathed it as a child with the parties my parents would have up until I was about 14. We would be sent up to our rooms before the parties started and lay in bed while music was blasted downstairs and the constant tramping up the stairs of countless people to use the one toilet.

The following morning, I would go downstairs with the smell of alcohol and cigarette smoke hanging in the air and glasses of every description piled up in the kitchen sink.

The best New Year's Eve memories for me were standing in Aintree hospital maternity unit with Lesley watching the fireworks as 1987 became 1988 then having to leave the hospital to just miss my youngest daughter Nicola being born, the first baby girl from Bootle born on New Year's Day in 1988 and the only birth I was not present at. I had only just left the hospital, the midwife saying nothing will happen for a while so you may as well go home. Lesley came down in the lift to see me off and ongoing back up again Nicola was on her way. I walked home from the hospital to Edinburgh Close in Netherton and on arriving a neighbour that was minding our three other children told me the news and how wonderful was it when Nicola gave birth to her own baby Bella on New Year's Eve 2024.

When me and Lesley first married we came up to Skelmersdale for New year and were in my grandads watching 'The Devil Rides Out' when my mother who was in the next door neighbour Charlie and Marge's house stormed in at 23.50PM

'Get in next doors now it's nearly midnight'

I said 'mum we are watching this film we don't want to go in Charlies'

'Get in there now'

Even as a married couple we were still ordered against our will to go into the neighbours for the chiming of Big Ben.

When my father was alive we would all go to my mother's on boxing day and when he passed away my mother attempted to keep the tradition going but it only lasted for about two years.

Our children would call to ours every Christmas morning and then all gather again at ours on-Boxing day and return for Nicola's birthday on New Year's Day.

Now our hearts are broken our family torn apart and we cannot celebrate our golden wedding anniversary without all of our children being there.

And as me and Lesley enter our twilight years and John Lennon ringing in our ears

'Another year over and a new one just began'

I suffered from depression and was prescribed Prothiaden but had terrible side effects when I decided to come off them but I needed to do something positive with my life. And so, in 1990 I became active again within the labour party and the local trades council. I became the secretary of the Bootle UD039 branch of UCATT the long serving secretary John had passed away and along with the branch treasurer Terry and chair Phil we attended Johns house in Sterrix lane to collect the branch books. John had membership books all the way back till about 1962 when it was the amalgamated union of carpenters and joiners and there in the UCATT membership books was Robert Brennan apprentice 0.50p.

I also became the assistant secretary of Merseyside Trades Union councils and later secretary of South Sefton Trades Union council.

During this period, the trades council were trying to re-establish a TUC unemployed centre so I was nominated by UCATT to the steering group.

I was also nominated by UCATT to the national conference which was a real honour as I was able to address conference as a delegate.

There was opposition to the centre in South Sefton from some of the other Merseyside and Cheshire center's predominantly because some of the South Sefton steering committee had been on the management committee of the former South Sefton centre. These colleagues were not involved in any way whatsoever with the financial matters and fully exonerated but it was mine and other trade unionist's opinion that is was not about governance but about there being less in the pot of TUC monies to support the centers.

We continued to fight the Merseyside and Cheshire Unemployed Centers combined committee for recognition with local Sefton TUC branches funding us directly. The colleagues that were associated with the former South Sefton centre received our full support but against our wishes they all stood down from the management committee after two years of fighting for recognition.

They decided that their stepping down was the only way forward but still no funding came from outside of our own affiliated Sefton trade union branches.

After we gained recognition I represented the South Sefton centre on a ten-day Northwest people march for jobs leaving Chester and zig zagging across the Northwest arriving in Blackpool to be met by Tony Benn and Arthur Scargill and their speeches of welcome lifted our hearts on what was a grey rainy day.

Me and Lesley took part in further marches one being a six-day march from Bradford to Blackpool to the Tory party conference and also a three-day march against pit closures.

I had read a book by Walter Hannington a member of the communist party who formed the National Unemployed Workers Movement in the 1930s and his book 'unemployed struggles' is a book that I would encourage all to read.

With every step taken on those marches I felt immense pride and though our march to raise awareness of unemployment could not compare with the 1930s hunger marchers I was doing something I was fighting back.

'Have you done any work in the last seven day'

'Yes, I have been campaigning against unemployment'

There heralded months of being persecuted, called in for frequent interviews and questioned over 'working' when I was a volunteer.

The unemployed marches I took part in were broadly supported by the public as we marched through successive towns. You would get the occasional shout from a passing vehicle 'get a fucking job' yes if only there were jobs you ignorant thick bastards.

Later when I was in the legal profession I would defend people accused of DWP fraud and represent hundreds of claimants appealing disability decisions.

The secretary of the Sefton centre Paul who became an Anglican priest was trying to procure funding through a European initiative during which an exchange visit was arranged with trade unionists from Cologne.

I noticed that on one occasion that Paul rang me at home there was a clicking sound and I said to Paul 'did you hear that' and he said 'I think someone is listening in' so we ended our call.

A few weeks later Paul informed me that he had held a telephone conversation with trade unionists in Italy and received a call from Special branch enquiring of aspects of his conversation.

Paul asked them how they had obtained the information given he had only spoken over the telephone with the Italian trade union.

I enquired of BT was my phone tapped and they told me that they do not know and any such matters would be outside of their control.

We received a visit later from trade unionists from Cologne and I gave one of them my Northwest peoples march for jobs t-shirt and we were having a great chat and drinks when a former Labour councillor said 'Whose round is it?' then followed it up with 'I think it's the krauts turn to get the ale in' We apologised to our German guests who shrugged of the comment.

I did the sign for the new South Sefton centre Trades Union Council Unemployed and Community resource centre that included the road of the people's march for jobs logo and we opened three days per week at St Thomas church hall in Seaforth providing free welfare rights advice.

Once a giant of a man who looked like one of the rugged old west mountain men came into the centre with his quite boisterous mongrel. He demanded sheets of paper and a pen and set about writing strange things about religion whilst his dog urinated everywhere. He told us he liked art and politics and had changed his name by deed poll to reflect his interests.

After questioning us about religion the universe and future world order he left leaving his scribbled drawings behind. A few weeks later he returned, the dog jumped up onto the desk and started running amok and urinating again as it ran around whilst he rummaged through paperwork to find his drawings from his earlier visit. He became quite irate when he could not find his papers and left threatening us with fire and brimstone.

A few days later he held up the local post office with a shotgun and that was the last we saw of him. We learnt later that he had been banned from visiting the then MPs Joe Benton's office because of his behaviour. I would like to record my special thanks to Joe and his assistant Anne for the support they gave to me throughout my time in office.

I remained with the centre from 1992 until 1995 when I resigned as I had commenced work in the legal profession with J. Keith Park Solicitors and would be working out of the former Deacon Goldrein Green office in Walton Vale with J Keith Park having taken over all of the legal aid work after Deacon Goldrein Green was closed.

I found the transformation from offering advice from a TUC centre to a Solicitors practice quite daunting at first but soon got to grips with it and was then doing most of the firms DWP appeal representation.

I have a former Sefton council legal officer Brian Gibson to thank for my start in the legal profession. Brian a former Major with the TA had spoken with James Keith Park about welfare rights advice and mentioned that I provided welfare rights advice. I was representing Sefton residents in housing benefit cases against Sefton council with declared interest and I was contacted directly by James Keith Park who interviewed me and that was that.

I thoroughly enjoyed working in Walton Vale which did hold many good memories for me. One morning Pat a labour party member who along with his wife Karen had travelled home to vote for me at the shortlist meeting for Orrell ward came into the office reception. Pat who was a service director for MIND and based at the acute psychiatric unit Stoddard House at Aintree hospitals asked if I could see patients on the ward who were having difficulties accessing disability benefits and financial problems. I attended each Friday and so began a long friendship with Pat who a year later offered me a position as an advocate with MIND. And I was accredited with formulating National MIND response to the then green paper on welfare reform.

A few funny things did happen when I was at J Keith Park Solicitors I had come back to the office from an appeal hearing in Dale street and walked in and every office plant had gone and these were specimen bamboo, cheese and Olive oil plants.

Apparently, a number of men clad in Green overalls came in and took them out and nobody thought to question it believing they were likely being replaced the same thing happened within the other two Solicitors practices on Walton Vale, all three practices left devoid of their specimen plants.

On another occasion one of the newly qualified executives purchased a large water colour painting of the Liverpool water front and the three graces and some guy walked in and took it off the wall and scarpered.

Another time someone scaled the rear of the building to try and break in the top floor window a feat only capable of being carried out by Spiderman

I was sent to Page Moss to cover, the office which was opposite the infamous Eagle and Child pub and every night at 16.00PM local kids would pull the shutters down trapping you inside till someone lifted them up.

One morning two lads came in and tried to steal the receptionist's computer though that happened at another practice in Netherton were I was based some years later but that computer was chained and went crashing to the floor.

I spent two years at MIND before returning to the legal profession with Kennan Benjamin Kay Solicitors first in their Walton Vale office which was the former J Keith Park Solicitors office then in Marian Square Netherton.

I was with them for seven wonderful years and was sent on training courses for mental health law and I continued to attend the MIND office and see detained patients.

Once community legal services came into being and the pie had to be shared out it was no longer financially lucrative for solicitors to do legal aid work and we would use all our allowance midway through the year and there is only so much pro-bono work you can do as a fee earner. The firm were looking for me to do personal injury and road traffic cases neither of which I had any interest in and an opening had arisen back at MIND so I left the legal profession. Kennan Benjamin Kay was one of the most supportive employers I worked for and gave me full support in my mayoral year 1999/2000 and I left them with heaviness in heart. There were again lots of hilarious memories one being the day I was asked if on my way back from the hospital could I call in at an address in Aintree to obtain instructions for a divorce.

The would-be client informed me that his wife 'is out getting pissed again so I need to sign the paper before she comes back'

I took the legal forms out of my case as his phone rang which he answered 'yes the solicitor is here now I'm signing the divorce papers'

I started to take his instructions when his wife came staggering in the room having come from the club opposite their home 'Divorcing me you fucking bastard' landing a punch on his head as he sat next to me.

'Get off me you are drunk I'm sick of you'

'Don't divorce me, I love you Billy (not his name) he then said 'and I love you'

They both turned around looked at me and said 'you get the fuck out of our house now'

I got back to Walton Vale and must have looked a sight the family lawyer in between laughing asked me if I was okay. I told him what happened and he said 'Did he sign the form first because we will still get paid'

Another funny tale that was relayed to me was when one of the solicitors now a Judge went to a house in Liverpool.

It was teaming down and a dog came hurtling across the field and was jumping up at him in a friendly manner and he kept batting it away with his brief case so as not to get muddy paws on his coat.

The door was opened and the dog ran inside, the guy who answered the door beckoned him into the living room where the dog was now laying curled up on a rug in front of the electric fire. The house apparently smelt heavily of cigarette smoke with a pyramid of cigarette stubs in the ash tray surrounded by several empty cans of McEwan's lager and on being offered a cup of tea he politely declined.

Next minute the dog got up and did a shit on the rug.

'Sorry' said the solicitor 'I will have to go'

The guy most annoyed said 'and take your fuckin dog with you'

I had two clients a brother and sister both with severe mental health problems who would turn up for appointments at Netherton and no matter who was in the reception area they would link arms and do the full 'Blue ridge mountains of Virginia' Laurel and Hardy dance act

Twirling each other around and taking a bow at the end.

It was funny and they would say to me 'Mr Brennan did you like that' I never laughed at them as mental health service users they were just so nice and the days of laughing at mental health patients should forever been consigned to the Victorian days but sadly the stigma persists. Once they came in with a young woman in her twenties and introduced her as their friend. I asked the friend to remain in reception and enquired of how this new friend had come to be and they informed me that she had offered to carry their shopping in Walton Vale and then said she would do all future shopping for them and held their benefit books.

They went on to tell me that this girl brought her friends around and they would turn up at the house all hours and just sit and watch TV. The sister said 'they smoke those drugs Mr Brennan and sometimes tell us to go to bed'

I immediately had the friend in reception removed off the premises and contacted the mental health nurses as an urgent safeguarding concern.

The matter was reported to the police after which they ceased to attend the home. Unfortunately, there was no prosecution of the 'friends' as the benefit books had willingly been handed over each week after signing the pages authorising someone else to collect the benefit for them.

This was a clear example of abuse and may well have been cuckooing.

Another funny occasion a client and members of his family sat in reception eating chips from the Bungalow chippie next door ignoring the sign 'no food to be consumed in reception' and enquiring if I had purchased my Christmas turkey which I had not and but that I would be getting one.

A few days later the client contacted me to tell me he had got me a large turkey only problem it was still alive.

It was later reported that a turkey farm had a number of turkeys stolen was the one obtained for me from that farm I don't know but I had already declined the offer.

Job Centre

My wife Lesley was made redundant from Rolls Royce and had to register as unemployed for the first time.

On attending the job centre a couple of questions were taken and a further appointment was arranged that she asked me to attend with her.

The following week we attended for her appointment and I informed reception that my wife had an appointment at 11.10AM, it was 10.50 AM and we were told to take a seat. At 11.30AM. I approached reception and said my wife had an appointment at 11.10AM do they know how much longer it will be to be told 'her appointment was upstairs' We went upstairs and the room was empty with one guy sat behind a desk. I told him my wife had an appointment at 11.10AM but we were sat downstairs.

Without looking up from his computer he said 'It's now turned 11.30AM she will have to make another appointment'

I said 'It is not her fault we were just told to take a seat not take a seat upstairs'

Again, without looking up from his computer he replied 'they would have told you to take a seat upstairs'

I said 'you cannot simply treat people this way' at which Lesley stood up and said 'come on let's go I'm never coming back here again it is degrading' Lesley never went back and a week later a letter arrived saying her benefit will be stopped if she does not sign on. The letter went straight into the bin and she never claimed a penny. I have heard of many such examples of people feeling humiliated at the job centre. However I have known exceptional trade unionists that worked within the civil service and were routinely moved for their support of campaigns against cuts in welfare benefits.

Orrell Ward 1994

I had no aspirations whatsoever to stand for elected office and was the local labour party branch ward secretary and heavily involved with the trade's council. The ward chairperson announced out of the blue that he was moving me against the incumbent councillor who was up for re-election and that was that.

The ward chair Terry stepped down after I was elected and said he had stayed long enough go see me take over as ward councillor which was immensely humbling for me. Later my friend and neighbour Kenny Jones a stalwart of the trade union movement and a former Bootle councillor became chair of the ward. Kenny was a magistrate and resigned from the bench during the poll tax years as he was not going to prosecute anyone brought before the bench for not paying the poll tax. Kenny was a true socialist and his daughter Carol told me on his passing of how her dad would refer to me as the best councillor that the ward ever had. What a compliment from such a great man, I must have been doing things right.

When first elected I was unemployed and immediately notified the DWP of the allowance that I would receive and up until I commenced work in the legal profession in January 1995.I would have the councillor allowances deducted at source from my welfare benefit less £20 that you were allowed to earn doing any work.

However, as a councillor you are not employed as you cannot be employed by any local authority that you are an elected member of and you only received an allowance not a wage so there posed the question how can you be treated as working? The allowances that you receive must be those reasonably incurred in the performance of your duties so you could claim for using your home as an office which I think equated to about £120 per annum.

As an unemployed councillor you are under the microscope in that you must be 'actively seeking work'

Before I became a councillor there was an attempt to discredit me in order to have me removed as the candidate.

I had allegedly informed on a DWP claimant having rang the DWP as Councillor Brennan to protest at this fraudulent claim.

I was a voluntary welfare rights adviser with the Trades council and the Merseyside association of trades councils instructed a leading barrister that took the DWP to task and it came out that it was malicious and I received an apology but as Mark Twain once said

'A lie can travel halfway around the world while truth is still putting on its shoes'

It did not stop the comments and graffiti in my neighbourhood and I just had to carry on doing what I was doing and people will eventually realise the truth behind it. The people behind it had underestimated the support that I had within the trade union movement and as a welfare rights adviser.

The DWP attended an interview with the leader of the labour group and were told that they had never spoken with me or seen me just received a phone call saying

'Im councillor Brennan from Sefton council Im reporting a DWP fraud'

The DWP on hearing from a councillor and without clarifying the details launched an immediate investigation, it was that simple.

I learnt several years later from a senior councillor of the identities of the architects of the campaign one of whom was involved in an alleged sexual relationship with the DWP claimant. The senior councillor who revealed the source stated that the two people behind it did so alone but had informed others of what they had done.

I came across further attempts to remove councillors and council workers based on trumped up charges. One such charge was levied at staff trade union representatives who were being dismissed for gross misconduct. The case involved alleged verbal abuse of council officers at the opening of the One Stop Shop in Bootle. Despite statements from police officers who were present at the opening confirming that they were unaware of any incident the officials were still sacked. The decision to dismiss was upheld and at a meeting of the Labour group and I raised the matter of the police being unaware but was told that because the mayor had said he had seen it then it must be true. The same mayor and his wife the mayoress were later during their mayoral year found guilty of benefit fraud with both receiving custodial sentences.

Another occasion when confidential planning information was leaked to the press and irrespective of there being around 20 members of the planning committee and the caller to the press being anonymous. It was decided that a certain councillor was behind it as the press said that he spoke with a broad Liverpool accent and the labour group were seeking to suspend him pending investigations meaning that he could not be selected.

The Labour party held a meeting in Bootle town hall on the Sunday morning. I addressed the meeting stating it was akin to a kangaroo court and given we did have two caucuses at that time there was only three of us that turned up out of about 15 to support our colleague who was not invited. The result being about 20 in favour of suspension with we three against and that's friends for you. If everyone had turned up we would likely have still lost by a few votes but that is irrelevant we were supposed to be comrades.

My first councillor surgery was held in the old Bootle day centre in Linacre lane next to what was the Orrell housing office.

I had called into the office to introduce myself and overheard one of the housing officers on the telephone passing on details of a tenants address to a former councillor and the officer had an incredulous expression on his face when I said

'Why are you giving tenants details to a former councillor'

The information was thus no longer imparted

I had two sisters arrive at my surgery one of whom was a single person in a four-bedroom house and they told me that the housing would not move her to smaller accommodation.

When I enquired why they both informed me that they had refused to engage in sexual activity as a guarantee of being re-housed.

I was gob smacked and did not know how to approach the matter being a new councillor but I never for one-minute thought they may have been misleading me as I was aware of similar shameful allegations in Skelmersdale.

I went to the housing office and just asked why was a single person in a four-bedroom house and pointed out that a two-bedroom house was available near to the other sister's home. If the refusal to move the individual was on grounds of rent arrears as I was not unsure if there were any then deductions of benefit could be applied to recover the arrears but for me the most important issue was that the four-bedroom house was freed up.

To cut a long story short she was moved the following week but regarding the allegations they did not want to pursue a complaint and I understand people's reluctance when faced with people in positions of authority and power.

146

One Christmas eve I was contacted by a distraught older couple whose boiler had broken. They had rung the housing emergency number and were informed that they use a kettle to boil water and an electric heater would be dropped off to them that they could move from room to room as there was no one available to affect the repair till the new year. I enquired if there was a boiler in another void property and if so that the part that was broken be taken from the void property boiler. I received a call from a senior housing officer who said that the part had to be ordered and I said if they knew what the part was then take it out of the void property Im not accepting anything less.

An engineer was sent out to remove the part from the void property and it was fitted later on Christmas eve.

Another occasion I along with the other two ward councillors were invited to a meeting in the town hall by the chair of planning. A developer had bought disused railway to use for a landfill close to my home. The chair of planning unfolded a large sheet of paper and the developer proudly told us that the only problem was access to the site but they had solved that.

He went on to say that they would knock down two houses on Harris Drive just after the allotments and that would be the entrance to the landfill operation.

I asked how could they just knock down two houses that they could not get a compulsory purchase order and they both said that the two houses would be bought for a reasonable price and then knocked down.

I pointed at the two houses on the map and said

'do you see that second house'

Yes, was the reply

'That is mine and you aint having it'

The chair of planning folded up his paper and walked out the room with the developer and that was the end of that.

When we bought our house there was a chap lived close by who despised councillors accusing each and every one of them of being corrupt.

He knocked on the door of the house we were buying to ask the vendor if we were paying cash for the house.

Cabinet

I think the worst thing to happen to local democracy was to bring in the cabinet structure and for the leader to appoint members of the cabinet. This destroys back bench councillors opportunities to debate matters and make decisions.

Having one person appoint positions paves the way for cronyism and nepotism and there is no structure to challenge such appointments.

The introduction of scrutiny & review committees is yet another failing of the democratic process as such review committees can only make recommendations.They cannot change cabinet decisions and are just plain and simple a 'paper toothless tiger'

How can it be democratic when you attend a meeting of the labour group and are told that the eight or nine councillors that make up the cabinet tell you what has been decided and you are expected to just follow.

How can it be democratic when the leader tells the group to prime questions for cabinet to take up all the time of council members question time.

In one disgraceful example 'get your questions in to cabinet members so there is no time for the opposition to ask me questions about children's service' followed by a chuckle.

This when the public are rightly concerned and seeking answers to a damning report on failings in Sefton children's services.

How can it be democratic when cabinet members response to opposition councillors are one-word answers 'yes' or 'no' and yet members of their own party are given responses that run into paragraphs.

Pigs with their snouts in the trough

Where there's muck there's brass and non-more so than the feeding frenzy of the council trough. Meritocracy you ask! how dare someone suggest positions should be allocated on one's abilities what poppy cock.

Hail to the leader for the leader is an omniscient being.

And so, people would be allocated positions on the basis of their personal and family ties and bums on seats and that is an undeniable fact. Sadly, once the have nots became the haves they too become pre-occupied with the lucrative rewards through the kissing of the ring.

A councillor who had joined the feeding frenzy at the trough was once worried about losing his position and his partner who also became a councillor said to me.

'It's not about the money Bob, but you get used to it'

My reply 'I wouldn't know'

I became chair of the board of Sefton New Directions a position I held for about 12 years before the trade union and another board member also a member of the cabinet learnt that there was never any special responsibility allowance (SRA) paid to the chair of the board unlike other outside board chairs and they both supported an SRA which was awarded for the final three years I was on the board till I resigned. A year before I resigned the board were seeking new directors with experience and were to pay an allowance of around £8k per annum and to increase the board chairs allowance to £10k.

I declined to accept the £10K as staff of the company had not received any pay increase and I requested the allowance remain the same as a council committee SRA.

The first decision I made on becoming chair was to appoint the trade union representative to the board with access to all papers.

I was told by the trade unions that the staff viewed me as the protector of their terms and conditions of employment and that I showed true leadership.

A façade of local politics is the public facing 'we are all one' but behind the scenes councillors are being de-selected not because they lack ability but because they carry out the very role that they are elected to do, represent the best interest of the electorate whether they voted for them or not.

Orrell Mount Park

My 28.6 years in politics ended abruptly in October 2022, though I was not due up for election again until May 2024.

The council were looking to rip up the green pitches on Orrell Mount which is a stone throw from my home and replace them with rubber crumb pitches and this was against the wishes of the community.

In fact, the council undertook a consultation exercise involving less than a dozen houses directly facing the field in what I later described as a 'sham consultation exercise'

All councillors me included from the two wards Netherton & Orrell where the park is located and neighbouring Litherland ward had ignored requests to meet with local residents that had formed a campaign group against the proposal.

Residents that stood outside the entrance in all weathers shamefully denied access to their elected representatives and for what? Because some dared stand against the labour party locally as they felt councillors were not listening to the community.

My close neighbours and friends were supporting the campaign to keep the park as it was and I could no longer justify ignoring my constituents and decided to meet with the residents and hear their concerns directly. I went across to the park, the only councillor to do so and met the campaign group all of whom welcomed the fact that I had met with them. I was posed several questions one of which was would I support the residents in their campaign.

I recall my time in Skelmersdale unemployed workers centre and the great work they did to alleviate poverty against a blanket refusal from the labour party to support the centre, why? because some of them had stood in local elections against Labour

'Sounds familiar'

On hearing the residents' concerns I gave a commitment to support the campaign and on the morning that bulldozers came to rip up the field I sent an urgent email to the legal department/planning officers expressing my concern at the lack of consultation and risks to the community from cacogenic material. I had been up all the previous night carrying out research and learnt that all rubber crumb pitches in the Netherlands were being ripped up and replaced with grass because of concern over cancer etc.

I informed the officers that they should halt all works until we had an independent report in to the risks and a wider consultation for at least a one-mile radius. I was not interested in the officers stating Sport England were supporting rubber crumb pitches I wanted independent research of any risks.

I made it quite clear that my legacy as a councillor was not going to be the future health concerns of local children and that a primary school was adjacent to the park.

There were several attempts to cut me out of the loop, on one occasion I informed the campaign group that I would notify them when the consultation period would commence only to find that information in a news article in the Liverpool Echo. I was incensed and apologised to residents whom naturally felt deceived and of course how could a councillor not know of the date. I sent an email to the leader and officers and I was informed that my not being told was an oversight. I made it quite clear that it was wholly unacceptable and issued a public statement to the residents through the campaign group.

I had also sent an email to the councillors from both wards and relevant officers that I cc the campaign group into in the interest of transparency.

That action led to my being reported to the whip but that was later withdrawn as I had not broken labour party rules however for me that was it.

I brought a complaint to the Labour party nationally that bounced back within a few hours 'as not meeting the Labour party complaints policy'

I re-submitted the complaint to the Labour party national chair and received an email acknowledging receipt and assuring me it would be sent to the complaints department. No further communication was ever received by me and that is a damning indictment of the Labour party.

I decided to resign my seat I could no longer remain in a group where my position as an elected member was being undermined because others refused to engage with members of the community which flies in the face of the Nolan Principles and the Local Government Association expectations of elected representatives.

That said if I had not of resigned when I did I would like to believe that I would have stayed true to my principles and resigned over the current broken promises and cuts that were not in the manifesto all of which is contributing to the rise in right-wing populism as an alternative.

I did a podcast regarding my resigning as a councillor after nearly 30 years of service and said that on supporting the residents and Orrell Mount park that I felt it was the first time that I had to take sides but that I had taken the right side and it was.

The person that unsuccessfully attempted to report me to the whip in the likely hope that I would be suspended had once said to me in a local branch meeting

'That people who cannot pay their mortgage should not be -re-housed'

This following my providing a councillor report on how local authorities can use the 'mortgage rescue scheme' to buy a property and allow a family to remain in the home and pay rent thus avoiding homelessness .I was taken a back and replied 'you call yourself a socialist' and 'people can fall on hard times for many reasons' and of course the meeting was abruptly closed down. I guess there was a target on my back ever since that meeting. There was once an instruction that if you had any complaints or dealings with One Vision Housing then it had to go through the same person who complained to the whip about me. I totally ignored the diktat and continued to represent my constituents' enquiries with One vision housing. With regard to the shenanigan's Im very much aware of ongoing complaints concerning allegations of malpractice and corruption some information that has not as yet been reported on that may eventually come within the public domain should future proceedings be brought and I shall leave it at that for now.

Reflecting on my support of others I once received a signed copy of the book The Shrewsbury Three by Jim Arnison regarding the imprisonment of building workers including Ricky Tomlinson for carrying out legitimate striker activity during the building workers strike in 1972 he wrote To Bob Brennan 'Don't let the bastards grind you down' a sentiment that is as relevant today as it was 50 years ago when the book was first published.

No Pasaran

They shall not pass, the slogan adopted by the republicans during the defence of Madrid during the Spanish civil war but first used in the first world war at the battle of Verdun in 1916. Being a proud anti-racist anti-fascist, I began researching fascism in the UK and the rise of Moseley's black shirts and the cable street battle of 04 October 1936. I then gained an interest in the international brigade during the Spanish civil war which history has taught us was a dress rehearsal for world war two.

I heard of the Jarama association and their attempts to have a memorial stone erected in Alcala De Henares where the bodies of hundreds of republicans and international brigade volunteers were disinterred and unceremoniously dumped into a pit that was then covered in tons of broken glass and then designated a rubbish dump making any future recovery impossible.

I contacted Walter Greenhalgh the secretary of the Jarama Memorial Association. Walter who was a member of the Communist party of Great Britain served as a machine gunner with the La Marseillaise Battalion XIV international brigade and a painter and decorator by trade sent me information on what they were seeking to achieve and it gave me the idea to write as a catholic to the Archbishop of Madrid to seek the church support for the memorial. I was surprised to receive a letter a few short weeks later concurring with the words in my letter asking that the memorial be allowed for peace and reconciliation.

However, Alcala De Henares was outside the jurisdiction of Madrid and I was given the contact for the Bishop for the area as the church now owned the land of the former rubbish dump and the resting place of the fallen. I further wrote and the response was also one of reconciliation so I sent both letters to Walter who thanked me for my assistance sending me a book of first-class stamps as a small token of the association appreciation.

My efforts did not contribute to the memorial being put in place as the planning was well progressed but I feel happy to have gotten the church to recognise the importance of reconciliation given the then civil war amnesia in Spain.

A small memorial was placed at the site by a former French International brigade volunteer.

I also liaised with Bill Alexander of the International brigade association and had our ward party donate to them as they were also seeking to have a memorial at the bridge over Jarama. However, given the political sensitivity the memorial would be one to the fallen of both sides, something that the Jarama memorial association were opposed to hence their own memorial in Alcala De Henares.

Jack Jones wrote in a letter from Barcelona in July 1938 regarding Britain and France reluctance to support the democratically elected republican government stating

'We believe that there can be no compromise between fascism and the democratic ideas for which we ourselves have come here to fight'

Just over 14 months later after years of appeasement the world was at war.

I pay tribute to those volunteers that travelled from my own ward Orrell

Percy Keegan from Fernhill Road

Harold Dwyer from Marmion Avenue

Albert McCabe from Gardner Avenue who was killed at Brunete

Mayor of Sefton

I was Mayor of Sefton in 1999/2000 the youngest Mayor ever at that time and the only one who was working full time. I had two great years as Mayor and did manage to do some positive work in seeking to modernize the role of Mayor. I signed a petition to stop the closure of a school for the blind, which led to press headlines.

Mayor breaks with tradition and supports campaign.

The civic officers were at pains to point out that the Mayor should be non-political and my response was that as first citizen I should lead by example and support the people of the borough which is what I was doing.

I attended Gdansk for the 60th anniversary of the opening shots of the second world war at Westeplatte and layed a joint wreath at the memorial with a representative of the German parliament and we dined with both the German and Polish presidents. It was a hectic few days culminating in a service of reconciliation in a church that was gutted during the war and the Israeli philharmonic orchestra played throughout the service.

I also layed a wreath at the Gdansk ship yard Solidarnosc memorial. The Mayor of Gdansk Pawel Adamowicz was fatally stabbed in 2019 whilst watching the finale of a Polish charity event. I also attended the signing of the twinning agreement between Sefton council and Fort Lauderdale and presented with the key to the city.

We arrived during the mayoral elections with the incumbent Jim Naugle becoming the longest serving mayor in the history of Fort Lauderdale.

It is stated on Wikipedia that though he was a Democrat he frequently supported Republican candidates and co-chaired George W Bush presidential campaign in 2000 prior to which he had supported Richard Nixon, Gerald Ford and Ronald Reagan and George Bush junior. He is known for being quite controversial particularly towards the LGBT community. We never had any time to discuss politics it was all about Sefton promoting tourism notably golf and economic development but was plain and simple a junket. The visit was fascinating from the arrival at Newark Liberty international airport to be met with astonishment with passport control officer aghast as I had no bodyguard being a mayor.

I do not know how many business cards I was given and the questions

'Do you know the Beatles?' 'not personally' I would reply

'Do you know Mrs Lawrence from York'

'No, I have not had the pleasure' was my reply

'Have you visited the palace' and of course I had attended the royal garden party and that was that

'Did you meet the queen'

'Did you see the crown jewels'

'No actually they are in the tower of London not in the palace'

When we arrived at Newark we had to take an onward flight in a thunderstorm to Miami then be picked up to take us on to Fort Lauderdale.

Unfortunately, due to the thunder storms and delays the welcoming party lift was cancelled as it was considered we would not arrive till the following day but that was never relayed to us. So, there we were a party of Brits stood outside Miami airport and we decided the only option was to get two Yellow taxis to take us onwards.

How much to go to Fort Lauderdale we asked?

It will be 80 dollars was the reply and as it meant 4 going in one cab and 3 in the other we thought that wasn't.

Suddenly the 80 dollar trip became one of 100 dollars per person and we were not going to argue with these guys and it was 2AM in the morning.

A day later three of us were up early and set off on a stroll to be told in no uncertain term on our return to the hotel that it was dangerous to be out walking by ourselves, that we could have been held up and worse.

During the mayoral year the mayor would host a few receptions one being for the press, the reserve forces and the clergy. I scrapped the clergy reception replacing it with one for the early years staff though it returned to the usual format the following year under the next mayor.

We would attend functions all over the borough and once attended the Ainsdale show but arrived late as we had come from an earlier function in Liverpool St Georges hall with the Bahai faith.

On arriving we were met by a rather frantic woman 'Mr mayor you are late, we are about to crown the rose queen' we had our two youngest children with us aged 11 and 9 and this woman said 'They will have to wait there with the attendant they cannot follow the procession'

Lesley who was mayoress   responded with
'well if they are not allowed in the procession then neither will we be taking part'

The woman stood there mouth open with a look of shock and then said
'Well hurry up then'

There was a large marquis that had plants for sale inside and as I was walking over the same woman said to me
'There is nothing in there that would be of interest to you Mr Mayor' when I said I like flowers she said
'Do you have a garden in Bootle'

When Lesley was looking at a collage another person said to her 'Don't you think they are lovely they were done by the local schools'

Lesley said 'yes my daughter has done them in school' to be asked
'Do they do them in Bootle schools?'

Lesley reply was 'of course after all it they are all Sefton schools'

I was approached by one woman who held out her hand

'Mr mayor so pleased to meet with you' as soon as I spoke she said

'Oh, you are from the Liverpool end' and I would say 'Yes, the South of the borough'

The mayor would greet the orange lodge as they marched from Litherland library to Seaforth station on 12 July and I was asked if I would want the deputy mayor to do with me being a Catholic. Apparently a former catholic mayor had declined and asked the deputy to do it, I was taken back by that and attended to wave off the order of nthe orange lodge.

I reintroduced the armed forces reception after covid as all receptions had been ended due to austerity and savings but I got the councillors to fund the reception each year from their own ward budgets with only one of 66 councillors objecting saying it was not what ward budgets were for.

I signed the first armed forces covenant in Sefton which was the first covenant to be signed out of all the Merseyside boroughs.

I was able with the help of the then director of Education Bryn Marsh to locate a school clock that featured in articles about Bootle and the blitz. The clock on the wall of Bedford Road school stopped working as the school as incendiary bombs began to fall.

I had the clock and a picture of it on the school wall placed in the foyer of Bootle town hall and now a lasting memorial to the civilian war dead and will forever be the most humbling single act of my time in office.

I shall conclude my mayoral memories with the installation in Bootle town hall in 1999 attended by my parents.

My brother in law Ronnie enquired of my father if he was proud of what I had achieved to receive the response

'Why, anyone can become mayor'

In the mayor's parlor there is a writing desk and people were leaving messages of congratulations on a sheet of paper that we later took home.

On reading those messages the following day one stood out, that being the message from my father that simply said

'Remember I did it first my way' my uncle Tony's words ran true.

HMP Liverpool

I did get to see the inside of that grim Victorian goal as a visitor when I was commissioned to deliver series of training lessons to offender representatives and prison listeners prior to the pandemic on behalf of the Merseyside prison mentoring service and during one visit I was shown the eerily cold former condemned execution cell.

A whole wing of the prison was destroyed during the German blitz on the night of 18 September 1941 killing 22 prisoners, the body of one of those unfortunates not found till 11 years later when rubble was being cleared. My mother said that you could hear the screams of those trapped within the prison as the high explosives fell all around. Whether or not that is true is not clear as my mother was only 5 years of age at the time of the blitz but the story has been passed down so maybe there is some truth in it and of course one whole side of the prison runs alongside the entry separating the houses in Bootle up to Hornby road, the destroyed wing was never rebuilt. The IRA once attempted to destroy one of the prison walls on 04 February 1939 during one of their earlier terror campaigns with the last execution taking place in August 1964. The prison once counted Lord Fenner Brockway founder of the campaign for nuclear disarmament and Robert Tressell writer of the Ragged trousered philanthropist as inmates. Robert Tressell was buried in a pauper grave along with several others and rests in the cemetery adjacent to the prison. His final resting place now rightfully deserving of its granite commemorative stone. And there it is the end of my first book, I will no doubt recall things later that I missed in the book but conclude with some of my childhood and teen memories.

Airfix model and soldiers
Observer books of British birds and British wildlife
Western TV series, did Wagon train ever get to California?
The Fugitive and David Janssen on the run for four long years
The Outer Limits and Journey into the unknown
The Beverley Hillbillies and Batman 'Ker Pow'
Dr Who the original with William Hartnell
Rawhide and rowdy yates played by Clint Eastwood

The prisoner
The Pink Panther
Monty Pythons Flying Circus
Radio Luxembourg
Radio Caroline
Football programmes and the Pink Echo
Playing kerbie on the street between the odd passing car
Collecting car registration numbers when not everyone owned a car
Challenging girls to American skipping
Hop Scotch and Lally O
Catching tiddlers though I was always grounded afterwards for being on the canal bank.
Crackerjack and Blue Peter
Top of the Pops though I shudder and cringe at some of the past shows
The sound of my Lambretta scooter
That first kiss to the sound of The Moody Blues 'Nights in White Satin' playing in the background.
Last but not least the many friend's past and present that shaped my journey.